VOCA 탄탄

2

기본

Happy House

이 책의 **구성과 특징**

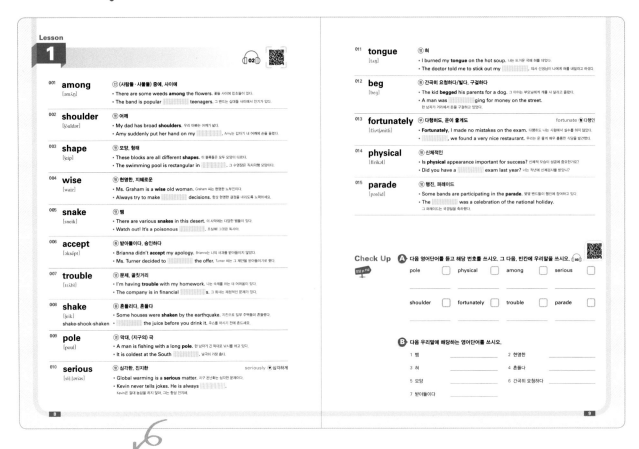

Lessons 1~30

- 각 레슨별로 15개의 단어를 학습합니다. 단어당 2개의 예문을 통해 단어의 의미와 용법을 보다 정확히 파악하고 빈칸에 직접 단어를 채워 써보며 익힙니다.
- MP3를 다운로드 받거나 QR코드를 통해 각 단어와 예문을 원어민 음성으로 듣고 정확한 발음을 익힐 수 있습니다.
- 해당 레슨에서 배운 단어들을 Check Up에서 간단히 점검합니다.

Workbook

해당 레슨에서 배운 단어들의 우리말을 떠올려 써봅니다.
그런 다음, 그 단어들을 반복하여 써보며 철자를 확실히 익히고 정리합니다.

Tests

총 3단계의 테스트(**Daily Test** → **Review** → **누적 테스트**)를 통한 체계적인 반복 학습으로 단어를 더욱 잘 기억할 수 있습니다.

• **Daily Test (온라인 제공):** 각 레슨을 학습한 뒤, 각 단어의 예문을 활용한 Daily Test를 통해 15개의 단어 공부를 마칩니다.

☆ 무료 다운로드 www.ihappyhouse.co.kr

• **Review:** 2개의 레슨마다 제공되는 Review를 통해 30개의 단어를 다양한 유형의 문제로 확인학습 합니다.

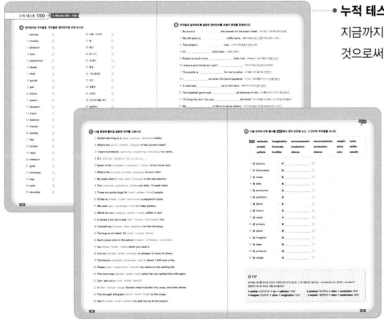

• **누적 테스트:** 10개의 레슨마다 제공되는 누적 테스트는 지금까지 배운 단어 150개, 300개, 450개를 총정리하는 것으로써 전체 학습을 마무리할 수 있습니다.

명사의 **복수형**

📓 **명사의 복수형을 알아봅시다!**

셀 수 있는 명사의 개수가 두 개 이상일 때 복수 명사라고 하며, 일반적으로 명사 뒤에 -s 또는 -es를 붙입니다.

① 명사의 끝에 '**-s**'가 붙는 경우

    e.g. book (책) – books   computer (컴퓨터) – computers
           dog (개) – dogs   pencil (연필) – pencils
           map (지도) – maps   son (아들) – sons
           house (집) – houses   umbrella (우산) – umbrellas

② 명사의 끝에 '**-es**'가 붙는 경우

    e.g. tomato (토마토) – tomatoes   bus (버스) – buses
           class (수업) – classes   dish (접시) – dishes
           box (상자) – boxes   watch (시계) – watches
    cf. photo (사진) – photos   piano (피아노) – pianos

③ 명사가 '**자음 + y**'로 끝나는 경우: y → i + -es

    e.g. baby (아기) – babies   party (파티) – parties
           city (도시) – cities   lady (숙녀) – ladies
    cf. toy (장난감) – toys   boy (소년) – boys

④ 명사가 '**f(e)**'로 끝나는 경우: y → v + -es

    e.g. leaf (나뭇잎) – leaves   shelf (선반) – shelves
           knife (칼) – knives   thief (도둑) – thieves
    cf. roof (지붕) – roofs

⑤ 단수 명사와 복수 명사의 **형태가 다른** 경우

    e.g. child (아이) – children   man (남자) – men
           woman (여자) – women   tooth (치아) – teeth
           goose (거위) – geese   foot (발) – feet
           mouse (쥐) – mice   antenna (곤충의 더듬이) – antennae

⑥ 단수 명사와 복수 명사의 **형태가 같은** 경우

    e.g. deer (사슴) – deer   sheep (양) – sheep
           fish (물고기) – fish   series (시리즈, 연속물) – series

⑦ 항상 복수형을 쓰는 명사

    e.g. pants (바지)   jeans (청바지)
           socks (양말)   shoes (신발)
           glasses (안경)   scissors (가위)

기수와 서수

📖 기수와 서수를 알아봅시다!

기수는 기본이 되는 수(1, 2, 3, 4 …)를 말하고, 서수는 순서를 나타내는 수(첫 번째, 두 번째, 세 번째, 네 번째 …)를 말합니다. 층수, 날짜, 기념일, 책 등을 이야기할 때 서수를 사용합니다.

e.g. My apartment is on the **6th (sixth)** floor.
We will visit Australia on August **24 (twenty-fourth)**, 2018.
Today is our **1st (first)** wedding anniversary.
I read the **4th (fourth)** book of the *The Lord Of the Rings* series.

숫자	기수	서수	숫자	기수	서수
1	one	first	16	sixteen	sixteenth
2	two	second	17	seventeen	seventeenth
3	three	third	18	eighteen	eighteenth
4	four	fourth	19	nineteen	nineteenth
5	five	fifth	20	twenty	twentieth
6	six	sixth	21	twenty-one	twenty-first
7	seven	seventh	30	thirty	thirtieth
8	eight	eighth	40	forty	fortieth
9	nine	ninth	50	fifty	fiftieth
10	ten	tenth	60	sixty	sixtieth
11	eleven	eleventh	70	seventy	seventieth
12	twelve	twelfth	80	eighty	eightieth
13	thirteen	thirteenth	90	ninety	ninetieth
14	fourteen	fourteenth	100	one hundred	one hundredth
15	fifteen	fifteenth	1,000	one thousand	one thousandth

CONTENTS

---

001 **among**
[əmʌ́ŋ]

전 (사람들·사물들) 중에, 사이에

- There are some weeds **among** the flowers. 꽃들 사이에 잡초들이 있다.
- The band is popular _____ teenagers. 그 밴드는 십대들 사이에서 인기가 있다.

---

002 **shoulder**
[ʃóuldər]

명 어깨

- My dad has broad **shoulders**. 우리 아빠는 어깨가 넓다.
- Amy suddenly put her hand on my _____. Amy는 갑자기 내 어깨에 손을 올렸다.

---

003 **shape**
[ʃeip]

명 모양, 형태

- These blocks are all different **shapes**. 이 블록들은 모두 모양이 다르다.
- The swimming pool is rectangular in _____. 그 수영장은 직사각형 모양이다.

---

004 **wise**
[waiz]

형 현명한, 지혜로운

- Ms. Graham is a **wise** old woman. Graham 씨는 현명한 노부인이다.
- Always try to make _____ decisions. 항상 현명한 결정을 내리도록 노력하세요.

---

005 **snake**
[sneik]

명 뱀

- There are various **snakes** in this desert. 이 사막에는 다양한 뱀들이 있다.
- Watch out! It's a poisonous _____. 조심해! 그것은 독사야.

---

006 **accept**
[əksépt]

동 받아들이다, 승인하다

- Brianna didn't **accept** my apology. Brianna는 나의 사과를 받아들이지 않았다.
- Ms. Turner decided to _____ the offer. Turner 씨는 그 제안을 받아들이기로 했다.

---

007 **trouble**
[trʌ́bl]

명 문제, 골칫거리

- I'm having **trouble** with my homework. 나는 숙제를 하는 데 어려움이 있다.
- The company is in financial _____s. 그 회사는 재정적인 문제가 있다.

---

008 **shake**
[ʃeik]
shake-shook-shaken

동 흔들리다, 흔들다

- Some houses were **shaken** by the earthquake. 지진으로 일부 주택들이 흔들렸다.
- _____ the juice before you drink it. 주스를 마시기 전에 흔드세요.

---

009 **pole**
[poul]

명 막대, (지구의) 극

- A man is fishing with a long **pole**. 한 남자가 긴 막대로 낚시를 하고 있다.
- It is coldest at the South _____. 남극이 가장 춥다.

---

010 **serious**
[sí(:)əriəs]

형 심각한, 진지한   seriously 부 심각하게

- Global warming is a **serious** matter. 지구 온난화는 심각한 문제이다.
- Kevin never tells jokes. He is always _____.
  Kevin은 절대 농담을 하지 않아. 그는 항상 진지해.

011 tongue

[tʌŋ]

몡 혀

- I burned my **tongue** on the hot soup. 나는 뜨거운 국에 혀를 데었다.
- The doctor told me to stick out my ▨▨▨▨▨. 의사 선생님이 나에게 혀를 내밀라고 하셨다.

012 beg

[beg]

통 간곡히 요청하다/빌다, 구걸하다

- The kid **begged** his parents for a dog. 그 아이는 부모님에게 개를 사 달라고 졸랐다.
- A man was ▨▨▨▨ging for money on the street.
  한 남자가 거리에서 돈을 구걸하고 있었다.

013 fortunately

[fɔ́ːrtʃənitli]

閏 다행히도, 운이 좋게도   fortunate 혱 다행인

- **Fortunately**, I made no mistakes on the exam. 다행히도 나는 시험에서 실수를 하지 않았다.
- ▨▨▨▨▨, we found a very nice restaurant. 우리는 운 좋게 매우 훌륭한 식당을 발견했다.

014 physical

[fízikəl]

혱 신체적인

- Is **physical** appearance important for success? 신체적 모습이 성공에 중요한가요?
- Did you have a ▨▨▨▨ exam last year? 너는 작년에 신체검사를 받았니?

015 parade

[pəréid]

몡 행진, 퍼레이드

- Some bands are participating in the **parade**. 몇몇 밴드들이 행진에 참여하고 있다.
- The ▨▨▨▨ was a celebration of the national holiday.
  그 퍼레이드는 국경일을 축하했다.

Check Up

정답 p.112

Ⓐ 다음 영어단어를 듣고 해당 번호를 쓰시오. 그 다음, 빈칸에 우리말을 쓰시오. 🎧03

pole ☐	physical ☐	among ☐	serious ☐
___	___	___	___
shoulder ☐	fortunately ☐	trouble ☐	parade ☐
___	___	___	___

Ⓑ 다음 우리말에 해당하는 영어단어를 쓰시오.

1 뱀	_____	2 현명한	_____
3 혀	_____	4 흔들다	_____
5 모양	_____	6 간곡히 요청하다	_____
7 받아들이다	_____		

---

016 asleep
[əslíːp]

형 잠을 자고 있는

• I fell **asleep** during the movie. 나는 영화를 보던 중에 잠이 들었다.
• Be quiet. The baby is _____ now. 조용히 해. 아기가 지금 자고 있어.

---

017 mistake
[mistéik]

명 실수

• Everybody can make a **mistake**. 누구나 실수를 할 수 있다.
• John made many _____s on the test. John은 시험에서 많은 실수를 저질렀다.

---

018 midnight
[mídnàit]

명 밤 12시, 한밤중

• Lauren woke up suddenly at **midnight**. Lauren은 한밤중에 갑자기 잠에서 깼다.
• I must come back home by _____. 나는 자정까지 집에 돌아가야 한다.

---

019 without
[wiðáut]

전 ~ 없이

• You cannot succeed **without** their help. 너는 그들의 도움 없이는 성공할 수 없어.
• We cannot live _____ water. 우리는 물 없이 살 수 없다.

---

020 pair
[pɛər]

명 (짝을 이뤄 함께 쓰이는) 똑같은 종류의 두 물건, 쌍

• I bought a new **pair** of shoes. 나는 새 신발 한 켤레를 샀다.
• How many _____s of socks do you have? 너는 양말을 몇 켤레 가지고 있니?

---

021 active
[ǽktiv]

형 활동적인, 적극적인

• The old man is 80 years old, but he is very **active**. 그 노인은 80세이지만 매우 활동적이다.
• I'm an _____ member of this club. 나는 적극적으로 참여하는 이 동아리 회원이다.

---

022 environment
[inváiərənmənt]

명 환경

• What should we do to save our **environment**? 우리는 환경을 보호하기 위해 무엇을 해야 할까?
• My school has a good learning _____. 우리 학교는 좋은 학습 환경을 가지고 있다.

---

023 main
[mein]

형 가장 중요한, 주된

• What is the **main** idea of the book? 그 책의 주제는 무엇이니?
• This is the _____ entrance to the building. 여기가 그 건물의 중앙 출입구이다.

---

024 polite
[pəláit]

형 예의 바른, 공손한

• It is not **polite** to whisper in front of others.
다른 사람들 앞에서 귓속말을 하는 것은 예의 바른 행동이 아니다.
• The waiters were _____ to the customers. 종업원들은 고객들에게 공손했다.

---

025 order
[ɔ́ːrdər]

명 순서, 명령, 주문 동 명령하다, 주문하다

• List the names in alphabetical **order**. 그 이름들을 알파벳 순서로 나열하세요.
• I'd like to _____ a pepperoni pizza. 저는 페퍼로니 피자를 주문하고 싶어요.

026 **upset**
[ʌpsét]

(형) 기분이 상한

- The mom was **upset** when her son spilled the milk again.
  그 엄마는 아들이 우유를 또 다시 쏟자 화가 났다.
- Sometimes small things make us ▨▨▨▨. 때로는 작은 일들이 기분을 상하게 한다.

027 **behavior**
[bihéivjər]

(명) 행동, 행위

- The scientist studies the **behavior** of birds. 그 과학자는 조류의 행태를 연구한다.
- Emily apologized for her bad ▨▨▨▨. Emily는 자신의 잘못된 행동에 대해 사과했다.

028 **gentle**
[dʒéntl]

(형) 온화한, (바람·파도 등이) 잔잔한

- The man's smile was **gentle** and soft. 그 남자의 미소는 온화하고 부드러웠다.
- The beach is famous for its ▨▨▨▨ waves. 그 해변은 잔잔한 파도로 유명하다.

029 **item**
[áitəm]

(명) (하나의) 품목, (개개의) 것

- Some **items** are displayed in the shop window. 몇몇 제품들이 쇼윈도에 진열되어 있다.
- Put your personal ▨▨▨▨s into the bag. 여러분의 개인용품들을 그 가방에 넣으세요.

030 **swallow**
[swálou]

(동) (음식 등을) 삼키다

- **Swallow** the pills at once. 약을 한 번에 삼키세요.
- The snake quickly ▨▨▨▨ed a frog. 그 뱀은 재빨리 개구리를 삼켰다.

Check Up

정답 p.112

A 다음 영어단어를 듣고 해당 번호를 쓰시오. 그 다음, 빈칸에 우리말을 쓰시오. 🎧05

swallow ☐	polite ☐	environment ☐	without ☐
pair ☐	mistake ☐	behavior ☐	item ☐

B 다음 우리말에 해당하는 영어단어를 쓰시오.

1 잠을 자고 있는 _____   2 온화한 _____

3 기분이 상한 _____   4 밤 12시 _____

5 활동적인 _____   6 순서 _____

7 가장 중요한 _____

A 다음 영어단어의 우리말을 쓰시오.

1 pole _____   2 midnight _____

3 shoulder _____   4 tongue _____

5 active _____   6 fortunately _____

7 wise _____   8 serious _____

9 main _____   10 snake _____

11 beg _____   12 behavior _____

B 우리말과 일치하도록 알맞은 영어단어를 써넣어 문장을 완성하시오.

1 The band is popular _____ teenagers. 그 밴드는 십대들 사이에서 인기가 있다.

2 List the names in alphabetical _____. 그 이름들을 알파벳 순서로 나열하세요.

3 Ms. Turner decided to _____ the offer. Turner 씨는 그 제안을 받아들이기로 했다.

4 I fell _____ during the movie. 나는 영화를 보던 중에 잠이 들었다.

5 _____ the pills at once. 약을 한 번에 삼키세요.

6 These blocks are all different _____s. 이 블록들은 모두 모양이 다르다.

7 Put your personal _____s into the bag. 여러분의 개인용품들을 그 가방에 넣으세요.

8 Some bands are participating in the _____. 몇몇 밴드들이 행진에 참여하고 있다.

9 The waiters were _____ to the customers. 종업원들은 고객들에게 공손했다.

10 Is _____ appearance important for success? 신체적 모습이 성공에 중요한가요?

C 다음 영어문장이 우리말과 일치하면 O, 그렇지 않으면 X를 쓰시오.

1 We cannot live without water. 우리는 물 없이 살 수 없다. (   )

2 I'm having mistake with my homework. 나는 숙제를 하는 데 어려움이 있다. (   )

3 My school has a good learning environment. 우리 학교는 좋은 학습 환경을 가지고 있다. (   )

4 Some houses were shaken by the earthquake. 지진으로 일부 주택들이 흔들렸다. (   )

5 The man's smile was upset and soft. 그 남자의 미소는 온화하고 부드러웠다. (   )

D 다음 문장을 듣고 문장을 완성한 후, 빈칸에 쓴 영어단어의 우리말을 쓰시오. 🎧06

1 My dad has broad _____s. → ....

2 Brianna didn't _____ my apology. → ....

3 A man was _____ging for money on the street. → ....

4 The _____ was a celebration of the national holiday. → ....

5 A man is fishing with a long _____. → ....

6 Be quiet. The baby is _____ now. → ....

7 You cannot succeed _____ their help. → ....

8 Sometimes small things make us _____. → ....

9 John made many _____s on the test. → ....

10 Watch out! It's a poisonous _____. → ....

11 I'm an _____ member of this club. → ....

12 The scientist studies the _____ of birds. → ....

13 What is the _____ idea of the book? → ....

14 What should we do to save our _____? → ....

15 The swimming pool is rectangular in _____. → ....

16 I burned my _____ on the hot soup. → ....

17 Did you have a _____ exam last year? → ....

18 I bought a new _____ of shoes. → ....

19 It is not _____ to whisper in front of others. → ....

20 The company is in financial _____s. → ....

21 I must come back home by _____. → ....

22 I'd like to _____ a pepperoni pizza. → ....

23 Ms. Graham is a _____ old woman. → ....

24 Global warming is a _____ matter. → ....

25 The beach is famous for its _____ waves. → ....

26 Some _____s are displayed in the shop window. → ....

27 The snake quickly _____ed a frog. → ....

28 _____, I made no mistakes on the exam. → ....

29 _____ the juice before you drink it. → ....

30 There are some weeds _____ the flowers. → ....

Lesson 3

031 noise
[nɔiz]

명 소음   noisy 형 시끄러운

- Do not make **noise** in the library. 도서관에서는 떠들지 마시오.
- What's the _____ coming from the ceiling? 천장에서 나는 시끄러운 소리는 무엇이니?

032 mud
[mʌd]

명 진흙

- We used **mud** to make pottery. 우리는 진흙을 이용하여 도자기를 만들었다.
- His boots were covered with _____. 그의 장화는 진흙투성이였다.

033 simple
[símpl]

형 간단한, 단순한

- The recipe for popcorn is very **simple**. 팝콘을 만드는 법은 매우 간단하다.
- Nora bought a skirt with _____ patterns. Nora는 단순한 무늬가 있는 치마를 샀다.

034 able
[éibl]

형 능력이 있는, 할 수 있는   ability 명 능력

- Derek is **able** to play the violin. Derek은 바이올린을 연주할 수 있다.
- Some birds are not _____ to fly. 어떤 새들은 날지 못한다.

035 plus
[plʌs]

전 더하기   접 게다가

- One **plus** two is three. 1 더하기 2는 3이다.
- This bag looks good. _____, it is cheap. 이 가방은 좋아 보여. 게다가 싸다.

036 announce
[ənáuns]

동 (공식적으로) 발표하다, 알리다   announcement 명 발표

- The scientists **announced** the results of their experiment.
  과학자들이 그들의 실험 결과를 발표했다.
- The winner of the contest will be _____d soon. 대회의 승자가 곧 발표될 것이다.

037 experience
[ikspí(:)əriəns]

동 경험하다, 겪다   명 경험

- I **experienced** back pain after the accident. 나는 사고 후에 요통을 겪었다.
- Ms. Brown has a lot of teaching _____. Brown 씨는 가르친 경험이 많다.

038 manner
[mǽnər]

명 방식/방법, 태도

- Keep stirring the soup in this **manner** for six minutes. 이런 식으로 수프를 6분 동안 계속 저어.
- Greet the guests in a friendly _____. 손님들을 친근한 태도로 맞이하세요.

039 shout
[ʃaut]

동 소리를 지르다, 외치다

- I heard somebody **shouting** my name. 나는 누군가가 내 이름을 외치는 것을 들었다.
- My sister _____ed at me to be quiet. 누나는 나에게 조용히 하라고 소리쳤다.

040 shade
[ʃeid]

명 그늘

- A man is sleeping under the **shade** of a tree. 한 남자가 나무 그늘 아래에서 잠자고 있다.
- Let's have lunch in the _____. 그늘에서 점심을 먹자.

041 **envelope**
[énvəlòup]

명 봉투

- Sam put some pictures in the **envelope**. Sam은 봉투에 몇 장의 사진을 넣었다.
- I wrote my address on the ▨▨▨▨▨. 나는 봉투에 내 주소를 썼다.

042 **thief**
[θiːf]

명 도둑

- A **thief** stole my purse. 도둑이 내 지갑을 훔쳐갔다.
- The ▨▨▨▨▨ was arrested by a police officer. 그 도둑은 경찰에 의해 체포되었다.

043 **goods**
[gudz]

명 상품

- The brand is known for its leather **goods**. 그 브랜드는 가죽 제품으로 유명하다.
- The clerks are displaying their ▨▨▨▨▨ for sale.
  점원들이 판매를 위한 상품들을 진열하고 있다.

044 **position**
[pəzíʃən]

명 위치/자리, 자세 　　　　　　　　　　　　　pose 통 자세를 취하다

- The moon changes **positions** from night to night. 달은 밤마다 위치를 바꾼다.
- You should change your sleeping ▨▨▨▨▨. 너는 잠자는 자세를 바꿔야 해.

045 **total**
[tóutl]

형 전체의　명 총합, 합계

- This book has a **total** of 200 pages. 이 책은 총 200페이지이다.
- I spent 90 dollars in ▨▨▨▨▨ at the store. 나는 그 가게에서 총 90달러를 썼다.

Check Up

정답 p.112

A 다음 영어단어를 듣고 해당 번호를 쓰시오. 그 다음, 빈칸에 우리말을 쓰시오. 🎧08

position ☐	goods ☐	manner ☐	able ☐
_____	_____	_____	_____
announce ☐	total ☐	experience ☐	envelope ☐
_____	_____	_____	_____

B 다음 우리말에 해당하는 영어단어를 쓰시오.

1 소리를 지르다 _____　　2 소음 _____

3 더하기 _____　　4 간단한 _____

5 도둑 _____　　6 그늘 _____

7 진흙 _____

15

046	**pan** [pæn]	몡 팬, 프라이팬

• Don't touch that **pan**! It's still hot. 저 팬을 만지지 마! 아직 뜨거워.
• I used a frying _____ to cook the bacon. 나는 프라이팬을 사용해서 베이컨을 구웠다.

047	**nest** [nest]	몡 새 둥지, (곤충 등의) 보금자리

• Some birds make their **nests** in the tree tops. 어떤 새들은 나무 꼭대기에 둥지를 짓는다.
• We found a big ant _____ in the forest. 우리는 숲에서 커다란 개미집을 발견했다.

048	**orchestra** [ɔ́ːrkistrə]	몡 관현악단, 오케스트라

• Kevin plays cello in the school **orchestra**. Kevin은 학교 관현악단에서 첼로를 연주한다.
• The musician wants to play with an _____. 그 음악가는 오케스트라와 협연하고 싶어 한다.

049	**alive** [əláiv]	혱 살아 있는

• The bug is not dead. It's **alive**. 그 벌레는 죽지 않았어. 살아 있어.
• I think Michael Jackson is still _____ in the hearts of fans.
나는 Michael Jackson이 팬들의 마음속에 여전히 살아 있다고 생각한다.

050	**prefer** [prifə́ːr]	동 더 좋아하다, 선호하다

• Which do you **prefer**, coffee or tea? 커피와 차 중에 어떤 것을 더 좋아하니?
• I _____ action movies to romance ones. 나는 로맨스 영화보다 액션 영화를 좋아한다.

051	**attention** [əténʃən]	몡 주의/집중, 관심

• Pay **attention** when you walk across the street. 길을 건널 때에는 주의하세요.
• It is not easy to hold children's _____. 아이들의 관심을 끄는 것은 쉽지 않다.

052	**explain** [ikspléin]	동 설명하다 explanation 몡 설명

• The teacher **explained** some rules to us. 선생님은 우리에게 몇 가지 규칙을 설명해 주셨다.
• Can you _____ why you're late? 너는 왜 늦었는지 설명해 줄래?

053	**mark** [maːrk]	동 표시하다 몡 자국, 흔적

• I **marked** my name on the book cover. 나는 책 표지에 내 이름을 표시했다.
• There is a dirty _____ on your shirt. 네 셔츠에 지저분한 자국이 있어.

054	**possible** [pásəbl]	혱 가능한

• Is it **possible** to buy the book online? 그 책을 온라인에서 구입할 수 있나요?
• Please answer me as soon as _____. 가능한 한 빨리 답변해 주세요.

055	**limit** [límit]	동 제한하다 몡 제한

• The school **limits** the class size to 20 students. 그 학교는 학급 규모를 20명으로 제한한다.
• Do not drive faster than the speed _____. 제한 속도보다 빠르게 운전하지 마시오.

056 trust
[trʌst]
⑧ 신뢰하다, 믿다   ⑲ 신뢰, 믿음
- Ellen is always honest, so you can **trust** her. Ellen은 항상 정직하니까, 그녀를 믿어도 돼.
- I have no _____ in you anymore. 나는 더 이상 너를 믿지 않아.

057 billion
[bíljən]
⑲ 10억
- The company spent **billions** of dollars on marketing.
  그 회사는 마케팅에 수십억 달러를 썼다.
- This world's population is over seven _____. 전 세계 인구는 70억이 넘는다.

058 grab
[græb]
⑧ 꽉 붙잡다, 쥐다
- The woman **grabbed** her baby to feed him. 그 여자는 아기를 꽉 잡고 우유를 먹였다.
- Please _____ your bag and follow me. 가방을 쥐고 저를 따라오세요.

059 president
[prézidənt]
⑲ (모임·회사 등의) 회장, 대통령
- Karen is the **president** of our book club. Karen은 우리 독서 동아리의 회장이다.
- Many people are supporting the new _____.
  많은 사람들이 새 대통령을 지지하고 있다.

060 treasure
[tréʒər]
⑲ 보물, 보물 같은 존재
- The boy found hidden **treasures** under the tree.
  그 남자아이는 나무 밑에 숨겨져 있던 보물을 찾았다.
- This doll is my daughter's _____. 이 인형은 내 딸에게 보물 같은 존재이다.

Check Up

정답 p.113

A 다음 영어단어를 듣고 해당 번호를 쓰시오. 그 다음, 빈칸에 우리말을 쓰시오. 🎧10

president ☐   billion ☐   attention ☐   pan ☐

_____   _____   _____   _____

orchestra ☐   possible ☐   explain ☐   treasure ☐

_____   _____   _____   _____

B 다음 우리말에 해당하는 영어단어를 쓰시오.

1 살아 있는 _____   2 제한하다 _____

3 새 둥지 _____   4 표시하다 _____

5 선호하다 _____   6 꽉 붙잡다 _____

7 신뢰하다 _____

Review

정답 p.113

A 다음 영어단어의 우리말을 쓰시오.

1 billion _____ 2 nest _____

3 announce _____ 4 goods _____

5 orchestra _____ 6 experience _____

7 grab _____ 8 position _____

9 president _____ 10 trust _____

11 possible _____ 12 treasure _____

B 우리말과 일치하도록 알맞은 영어단어를 써넣어 문장을 완성하시오.

1 The school _____s the class size to 20 students. 그 학교는 학급 규모를 20명으로 <u>제한한다</u>.

2 A man is sleeping under the _____ of a tree. 한 남자가 나무 <u>그늘</u> 아래에서 잠자고 있다.

3 Sam put some pictures in the _____. Sam은 봉투에 몇 장의 사진을 넣었다.

4 The recipe for popcorn is very _____. 팝콘을 만드는 법은 매우 <u>간단하다</u>.

5 My sister _____ed at me to be quiet. 누나는 나에게 조용히 하라고 <u>소리쳤다</u>.

6 Greet the guests in a friendly _____. 손님들을 친근한 <u>태도로</u> 맞이하세요.

7 This book has a _____ of 200 pages. 이 책은 <u>총</u> 200페이지이다.

8 A _____ stole my purse. <u>도둑이</u> 내 지갑을 훔쳐갔다.

9 We used _____ to make pottery. 우리는 <u>진흙을</u> 이용하여 도자기를 만들었다.

10 One _____ two is three. 1 <u>더하기</u> 2는 3이다.

C 다음 영어문장이 우리말과 일치하면 O, 그렇지 않으면 X를 쓰시오.

1 I marked my name on the book cover. 나는 책 표지에 내 이름을 표시했다. (   )

2 The teacher explained some rules to us. 선생님은 우리에게 몇 가지 규칙을 설명해 주셨다. (   )

3 Do not make attention in the library. 도서관에서 떠들지 마시오. (   )

4 Which do you prefer, coffee or tea? 커피와 차 중에 어떤 것을 더 좋아하니? (   )

5 Derek is alive to play the violin. Derek은 바이올린을 연주할 수 있다. (   )

D 다음 문장을 듣고 문장을 완성한 후, 빈칸에 쓴 영어단어의 우리말을 쓰시오. 🎧 11

1 Karen is the _____ of our book club.
→ ....

2 I wrote my address on the _____.
→ ....

3 Some birds make their _____s in the tree tops.
→ ....

4 What's the _____ coming from the ceiling?
→ ....

5 Some birds are not _____ to fly.
→ ....

6 Kevin plays cello in the school _____.
→ ....

7 Can you _____ why you're late?
→ ....

8 His boots were covered with _____.
→ ....

9 I heard somebody _____ing my name.
→ ....

10 Please answer me as soon as _____.
→ ....

11 The _____ was arrested by a police officer.
→ ....

12 There is a dirty _____ on your shirt.
→ ....

13 Nora bought a skirt with _____ patterns.
→ ....

14 I think Michael Jackson is still _____ in the hearts of fans.
→ ....

15 The woman _____bed her baby to feed him.
→ ....

16 The brand is known for its leather _____.
→ ....

17 Keep stirring the soup in this _____ for six minutes.
→ ....

18 Let's have lunch in the _____.
→ ....

19 The moon changes _____s from night to night.
→ ....

20 I _____ action movies to romance ones.
→ ....

21 I spent 90 dollars in _____ at the store.
→ ....

22 It is not easy to hold children's _____.
→ ....

23 This bag looks good. _____, it is cheap.
→ ....

24 This world's population is over seven _____
→ ....

25 The scientists _____d the results of their experiment.
→ ....

26 Don't touch that _____! It's still hot.
→ ....

27 Do not drive faster than the speed _____.
→ ....

28 Ellen is always honest, so you can _____ her.
→ ....

29 The boy found hidden _____s under the tree.
→ ....

30 I _____d back pain after the accident.
→ ....

061 **blow**
[blou]
blow-blew-blown

(동) 바람이 불다, 입으로 불다
- A strong wind is **blowing** from the west. 강한 바람이 서쪽에서 불어오고 있다.
- I ⬜⬜⬜ out the candles on the birthday cake. 나는 생일 케이크의 촛불을 불어서 껐다.

062 **award**
[əwɔ́ːrd]

(명) 상   (동) (상 등을) 주다, 수여하다
- I can't believe that I won the **award**! 내가 상을 타다니 믿을 수가 없어!
- They ⬜⬜⬜ed Luke a gold medal. 그들은 Luke에게 금메달을 수여했다.

063 **strange**
[streindʒ]

(형) 이상한   stranger (명) 낯선 사람
- I had a **strange** dream last night. 나는 어젯밤에 이상한 꿈을 꾸었다.
- The engine is making a ⬜⬜⬜ sound. 엔진에서 이상한 소리가 난다.

064 **although**
[ɔːlðóu]

(접) 비록 ~이지만
- **Although** it was raining, we still went out. 비가 오고 있었지만 우리는 밖으로 나갔다.
- ⬜⬜⬜ it was expensive, I bought the watch.
  그 시계는 매우 비쌌지만 나는 그것을 샀다.

065 **maybe**
[méibiː]

(부) 아마, 어쩌면
- **Maybe** it will snow tomorrow. 아마 내일은 눈이 올 거야.
- ⬜⬜⬜ Molly didn't tell the truth. 어쩌면 Molly는 사실을 말하지 않았어.

066 **avoid**
[əvɔ́id]

(동) ~가 발생하는 것을 막다, 사람을 피하다
- A driver must be careful to **avoid** accidents. 운전자는 사고를 막기 위해 신중해야 한다.
- Why are you often ⬜⬜⬜ing me? 너는 왜 자꾸 나를 피하는 거니?

067 **favor**
[féivər]

(명) 부탁, 도움, 호의
- Can I ask you a **favor**? 부탁 좀 해도 될까요?
- I owe Brian a ⬜⬜⬜. 나는 Brian에게 도움을 받은 적이 있다.

068 **master**
[mǽstər]

(명) 주인, 달인/대가   (동) 완전히 익히다, 통달하다
- The dog always follows its **master**. 그 개는 항상 주인을 따라다닌다.
- It is not easy to ⬜⬜⬜ a foreign language. 외국어를 완전히 익히는 것은 쉽지 않다.

069 **post**
[poust]

(동) 게시하다, (편지 등을) 부치다
- Mr. Turner **posted** a notice on the wall. Turner 씨는 벽에 공지 사항을 게시했다.
- Don't forget to ⬜⬜⬜ this letter. 이 편지를 부치는 것을 잊지 마세요.

070 **share**
[ʃɛər]

(동) 공유하다
- Jessica **shares** a bedroom with her sister. Jessica는 여동생과 침실을 같이 쓴다.
- Can I ⬜⬜⬜ this table with you? 테이블을 같이 써도 될까요?

071 unique
[ju:ní:k]

(형) 독특한, 유일한/하나뿐인
- This flower has a **unique** smell. 이 꽃은 독특한 향기가 난다.
- Everyone has a _____ fingerprint. 모든 사람은 하나뿐인 지문을 가지고 있다.

072 blossom
[blásəm]

(명) 꽃 (동) 꽃이 피다
- Yeouido is famous for its cherry **blossoms**. 여의도는 벚꽃으로 유명하다.
- The apple tree will start to _____ soon. 사과나무에 곧 꽃이 피기 시작할 것이다.

073 handle
[hǽndl]

(명) 손잡이 (동) 손으로 만지다/다루다, (상황 등을) 처리하다
- Turn the **handle** to open the door. 손잡이를 돌려서 문을 여세요.
- Broken bottles must be _____d carefully. 깨진 병은 조심히 다뤄져야 한다.

074 cancel
[kǽnsəl]

(동) 취소하다
- The baseball game was **canceled** because of the weather.
  날씨 때문에 야구 경기가 취소되었다.
- Can I _____ my order? I changed my mind.
  제 주문을 취소할 수 있나요? 생각이 바뀌었어요.

075 typical
[típikəl]

(형) 전형적인, 보통의   typically (부) 전형적으로, 보통
- A **typical** Korean meal includes rice, soup, and side dishes.
  전형적인 한국 식사에는 밥, 국, 그리고 반찬들이 포함된다.
- _____ teenagers care about their appearance. 보통의 십대들은 외모에 신경을 쓴다.

Check Up

정답 p.113

A 다음 영어단어를 듣고 해당 번호를 쓰시오. 그 다음, 빈칸에 우리말을 쓰시오. 🎧 13

post ☐	favor ☐	master ☐	avoid ☐
although ☐	typical ☐	handle ☐	blossom ☐

B 다음 우리말에 해당하는 영어단어를 쓰시오.

1 이상한 _____   2 아마 _____

3 독특한 _____   4 취소하다 _____

5 공유하다 _____   6 (상 등을) 주다 _____

7 바람이 불다 _____

Lesson 6

076 count
[kaunt]

동 (숫자의 합을) 세다

- I **counted** the coins and put them into my pocket. 나는 동전의 수를 세고 주머니에 넣었다.
- Do you _____ sheep to fall asleep? 너는 잠들기 위해서 양을 세니?

077 occur
[əkə́ːr]

동 발생하다, 일어나다

- A big flood **occurred** in India yesterday. 어제 인도에서 큰 홍수가 발생했다.
- An earthquake can _____ anywhere on Earth. 지진은 지구 어디에서나 일어날 수 있다.

078 price
[prais]

명 가격

- What's the **price** of the concert ticket? 그 콘서트 표의 가격은 얼마인가요?
- The _____ of the necklace is too high. 그 목걸이의 가격은 너무 높다.

079 argue
[áːrgjuː]

동 말로 다투다, 주장하다

- The brothers always **argue** with each other. 그 형제는 항상 서로 말다툼을 한다.
- The man _____d that the plans were wrong.
  그 남자는 그 계획이 잘못되었다고 주장했다.

080 relax
[rilǽks]

동 쉬다, 진정하다

- Let's just sit down and **relax** for a minute. 앉아서 잠시 쉬자.
- Classical music can help you _____. 클래식 음악은 진정하는 데 도움이 될 수 있다.

081 balance
[bǽləns]

명 균형 동 균형을 잡다

- Olivia lost her **balance** and fell down. Olivia는 균형을 잃고 넘어졌다.
- It can be difficult to _____ on one leg. 한쪽 다리로 균형을 잡기는 어려울 수 있다.

082 few
[fjuː]

형 (수가) 거의 없는

- There are **few** students at school on weekends. 주말에는 학교에 학생들이 거의 없다.
- _____ people were late to the party. 파티에 늦은 사람은 거의 없었다.

083 matter
[mǽtər]

명 (처리해야 할) 문제, 일 동 문제가 되다, 중요하다

- The **matter** should be solved quickly. 그 문제는 빨리 해결되어야 한다.
- It doesn't _____ who will go there. 누가 거기에 갈 것인지는 중요하지 않다.

084 praise
[preiz]

동 칭찬하다 명 칭찬, 찬사

- The teacher **praised** Leah for her kindness. 선생님은 Leah의 친절함을 칭찬하셨다.
- His latest novel is receiving high _____. 그의 최신 소설은 많은 찬사를 받고 있다.

085 shine
[ʃain]
shine-shone-shone

동 빛나다, 광을 내다   shiny 형 빛나는

- Millions of stars are **shining** brightly in the sky. 하늘에 수백만 개의 별들이 빛나고 있다.
- Mr. White _____s his shoes every day. White 씨는 매일 자신의 구두를 닦는다.

086 **tough**
[tʌf]

혱 매우 어려운, (음식이) 질긴, (사람이) 거친

• My teenage years were very **tough**. 나의 십대 시절은 매우 힘들었다.
• This meat is too _____. I can't eat it. 이 고기는 너무 질겨. 먹을 수가 없어.

---

087 **border**
[bɔ́:rdər]

몡 국경, 경계

• Niagara Falls is on the **border** of Canada and America.
  나이아가라 폭포는 캐나다와 미국 국경 지역에 있다.
• We built a fence along the _____ of the yard.
  우리는 마당 경계를 따라 울타리를 세웠다.

---

088 **harm**
[hɑ:rm]

몡 피해 동 해를 끼치다   harmful 혱 해로운

• The drought did great **harm** to the crops. 가뭄은 작물에 큰 피해를 입혔다.
• The dog will not _____ you at all. 그 개는 너를 전혀 해치지 않을 거야.

---

089 **provide**
[prəváid]

동 제공하다, 주다

• We **provided** poor people with food and clothes.
  우리는 가난한 사람들에게 음식과 옷을 제공했다.
• Drinks will be _____d for free at the event. 그 행사에서는 음료가 무료로 제공될 것이다.

---

090 **reason**
[rí:zən]

몡 이유

• What's the **reason** for the party? 파티를 하는 이유가 무엇이니?
• The baby started crying without any _____s. 아기가 아무런 이유 없이 울기 시작했다.

Check Up 정답 p.113

A 다음 영어단어를 듣고 해당 번호를 쓰시오. 그 다음, 빈칸에 우리말을 쓰시오. 🎧15

balance ☐	matter ☐	praise ☐	occur ☐
_____	_____	_____	_____

border ☐	tough ☐	provide ☐	argue ☐
_____	_____	_____	_____

B 다음 우리말에 해당하는 영어단어를 쓰시오.

1 거의 없는 _____   2 빛나다 _____

3 (숫자의 합을) 세다 _____   4 쉬다 _____

5 이유 _____   6 피해 _____

7 가격 _____

Ⓐ 다음 영어단어의 우리말을 쓰시오.

1 provide _____   2 border _____

3 strange _____   4 cancel _____

5 few _____   6 praise _____

7 post _____   8 blow _____

9 matter _____   10 count _____

11 avoid _____   12 balance _____

Ⓑ 우리말과 일치하도록 알맞은 영어단어를 써넣어 문장을 완성하시오.

1 The _____ of the necklace is too high. 그 목걸이의 가격은 너무 높다.

2 What's the _____ for the party? 파티를 하는 이유가 무엇이니?

3 Turn the _____ to open the door. 손잡이를 돌려서 문을 여세요.

4 The brothers always _____ with each other. 그 형제는 항상 서로 말다툼을 한다.

5 Can I ask you a _____? 부탁 좀 해도 될까요?

6 The drought did great _____ to the crops. 가뭄은 작물에 큰 피해를 입혔다.

7 I can't believe that I won the _____! 내가 상을 타다니 믿을 수가 없어!

8 _____ it will snow tomorrow. 아마 내일은 눈이 올 거야.

9 Jessica _____s a bedroom with her sister. Jessica는 여동생과 침실을 같이 쓴다.

10 _____ teenagers care about their appearance. 보통의 십대들은 외모에 신경을 쓴다.

Ⓒ 다음 영어문장이 우리말과 일치하면 O, 그렇지 않으면 X를 쓰시오.

1 This meat is too unique. I can't eat it. 이 고기는 너무 질겨. 먹을 수가 없어. (   )

2 Although it was raining, we still went out. 비가 오고 있었지만 우리는 밖으로 나갔다. (   )

3 A big flood occurred in India yesterday. 어제 인도에서 큰 홍수가 발생했다. (   )

4 The dog always follows its blossom. 그 개는 항상 주인을 따라다닌다. (   )

5 Let's just sit down and shine for a minute. 앉아서 잠시 쉬자. (   )

1 The baby started crying without any _____s. ➔ ....

2 We built a fence along the _____ of the yard. ➔ ....

3 His latest novel is receiving high _____. ➔ ....

4 A driver must be careful to _____ accidents. ➔ ....

5 Mr. White _____s his shoes every day. ➔ ....

6 It doesn't _____ who will go there. ➔ ....

7 A strong wind is _____ing from the west. ➔ ....

8 There are _____ students at school on weekends. ➔ ....

9 _____ Molly didn't tell the truth. ➔ ....

10 My teenage years were very _____. ➔ ....

11 Olivia lost her _____ and fell down. ➔ ....

12 _____ it was expensive, I bought the watch. ➔ ....

13 They _____ed Luke a gold medal. ➔ ....

14 I had a _____ dream last night. ➔ ....

15 The dog will not _____ you at all. ➔ ....

16 A _____ Korean meal includes rice, soup, and side dishes. ➔ ....

17 An earthquake can _____ anywhere on Earth. ➔ ....

18 I owe Brian a _____. ➔ ....

19 Can I _____ my order? I changed my mind. ➔ ....

20 Mr. Turner _____ed a notice on the wall. ➔ ....

21 Classical music can help you _____. ➔ ....

22 Broken bottles must be _____d carefully. ➔ ....

23 The man _____d that the plans were wrong. ➔ ....

24 I _____ed the coins and put them into my pocket. ➔ ....

25 What's the _____ of the concert ticket? ➔ ....

26 The apple tree will start to _____ soon. ➔ ....

27 Can I _____ this table with you? ➔ ....

28 It is not easy to _____ a foreign language. ➔ ....

29 This flower has a _____ smell. ➔ ....

30 Drinks will be _____d for free at the event. ➔ ....

091 pond
[pɑnd]

(명)연못

- The **pond** is very deep. Don't swim there. 그 연못은 매우 깊어. 그곳에서 수영하지 마.
- There were many frogs in the _____. 그 연못에는 많은 개구리들이 있었다.

092 outdoor
[áutdɔ̀ːr]

(형)야외의

- I like **outdoor** activities like trekking. 나는 트레킹과 같은 야외 활동을 좋아한다.
- The resort has two _____ swimming pools. 그 리조트에는 두 개의 야외 수영장이 있다.

093 spend
[spend]
spend-spent-spent

(동)(시간·돈을) 쓰다, 소비하다

- The man **spent** the weekend watching TV. 그 남자는 TV를 보며 주말을 보냈다.
- I _____ more than 100 dollars on shoes. 나는 신발을 사는 데 100달러 이상을 썼다.

094 arrow
[ǽrou]

(명)화살, 화살표

- Archers fight with bows and **arrows**. 궁수는 활과 화살을 가지고 싸운다.
- Follow the _____s to the event spot. 화살표를 따라 행사 장소로 가십시오.

095 reply
[riplái]

(명)대답 (동)대답하다, 답장하다

- I didn't get any **reply** from Chelsea. 나는 Chelsea에게서 어떤 대답도 듣지 못했다.
- You must _____ to the letter right now. 너는 지금 당장 그 편지에 대한 답장을 써야 해.

096 bark
[bɑːrk]

(동)(개 등이) 짖다

- The dog suddenly started **barking** at me. 그 개는 갑자기 나를 향해 짖기 시작했다.
- My dog only _____s at strangers. 우리 개는 낯선 사람에게만 짖는다.

097 flash
[flæʃ]

(명)번쩍임 (동)번쩍이다

- I just saw a **flash** of lightning. 나는 방금 번개가 번쩍이는 것을 보았다.
- The sunlight was _____ing on the water. 햇빛이 수면에 반짝거리고 있었다.

098 mayor
[méiər]

(명)시장

- Who is the **mayor** of your city? 당신이 사는 도시의 시장은 누구인가요?
- The citizens elected Ms. Hudson _____. 시민들은 Hudson 씨를 시장으로 뽑았다.

099 prepare
[pripέər]

(동)준비하다, 마련하다   preparation (명)준비

- All students are busy **preparing** for the exams. 모든 학생들이 시험을 준비하느라 바쁘다.
- My mom _____d meals for us. 엄마는 우리를 위해 식사를 마련해 주셨다.

100 pollution
[pəljúːʃən]

(명)오염   pollute (동)오염시키다

- Air **pollution** is a serious problem in China. 중국에서 대기 오염은 심각한 문제이다.
- Water _____ affects rivers, lakes, and oceans.
  수질 오염은 강, 호수, 그리고 바다에 영향을 미친다.

101 **volume**
[váljuːm]

ⓝ 소리 크기, 볼륨

- Please turn up the **volume** on the TV. TV 볼륨을 높여 주세요.
- The radio ⬚⬚⬚ was too loud. 라디오 소리가 너무 컸다.

102 **bother**
[báðər]

ⓥ 신경을 쓰다, 귀찮게 하다

- Don't **bother** to pick me up at the airport. 저를 데리러 공항에 나오지 않으셔도 돼요.
- You should not ⬚⬚⬚ your brother when he is studying.
  너는 형이 공부할 때 형을 귀찮게 해서는 안 돼.

103 **horror**
[hɔ́(ː)rər]

ⓝ 공포   horrible ⓐ무서운, 끔찍한

- Joshua loves **horror** movies about ghosts. Joshua는 귀신이 나오는 공포 영화를 좋아한다.
- I cried out in ⬚⬚⬚ when I saw the monster. 나는 괴물을 보고 공포에 질려서 울었다.

104 **purpose**
[pə́ːrpəs]

ⓝ 목적

- What's the **purpose** of your visit? 당신의 방문 목적은 무엇인가요?
- I'll go to Canada for the ⬚⬚⬚ of studying English.
  나는 영어를 공부할 목적으로 캐나다에 갈 것이다.

105 **usual**
[júːʒuəl]

ⓐ 평상시의, 보통의   usually ⓟ보통

- I arrived at school earlier than **usual**. 나는 평소보다 일찍 학교에 도착했다.
- It is not ⬚⬚⬚ for me to eat so much. 나는 평소에 과식을 잘 하지 않는다.

Check Up

정답 p.114

Ⓐ 다음 영어단어를 듣고 해당 번호를 쓰시오. 그 다음, 빈칸에 우리말을 쓰시오. 🎧18

usual ☐	outdoor ☐	volume ☐	reply ☐
_____	_____	_____	_____
flash ☐	purpose ☐	bother ☐	pollution ☐
_____	_____	_____	_____

Ⓑ 다음 우리말에 해당하는 영어단어를 쓰시오.

1 연못 _____   2 시장 _____

3 공포 _____   4 준비하다 _____

5 화살 _____   6 (개 등이) 짖다 _____

7 (시간·돈을) 쓰다 _____

106	**degree** [digríː]	몡 (각도·온도의) 도, 학위

• The temperature this morning is 17 **degrees**. 오늘 아침 기온은 17도이다.
• Mr. Green has a ＿＿＿＿＿ in physics. Green 씨는 물리학 학위를 가지고 있다.

107	**own** [oun]	동 소유하다　형 자기 자신의　　　　owner 몡 주인, 소유자

• Who **owns** the tallest building in the country? 누가 그 나라에서 가장 높은 건물을 갖고 있니?
• Everyone has his or her ＿＿＿＿＿ personality. 모든 사람은 자신만의 성격을 가지고 있다.

108	**stick** [stik] stick-stuck-stuck	몡 막대기　동 찌르다, 붙이다

• The old man uses a **stick** to walk. 그 노인은 지팡이를 사용해서 걷는다.
• The chef ＿＿＿＿＿ the knife into the pumpkin. 요리사는 호박에 칼을 찔러 넣었다.

109	**attack** [ətǽk]	동 공격하다　몡 공격

• A lion is **attacking** zebras. 사자 한 마리가 얼룩말들을 공격하고 있다.
• A young general led the ＿＿＿＿＿ on the town.
한 젊은 장군이 그 마을에 대한 공격을 이끌었다.

110	**rhythm** [ríðəm]	몡 리듬

• Let's dance to the **rhythm** of the music. 음악의 리듬에 맞춰 춤을 추자.
• The song starts with a slow ＿＿＿＿＿. 그 노래는 느린 리듬으로 시작한다.

111	**beat** [biːt] beat-beat-beaten	동 (경기 등에서) 이기다, 때리다/두드리다　몡 박자, 비트

• Nicole **beat** me in the race. Nicole이 경주에서 나를 이겼다.
• The drummer never misses a ＿＿＿＿＿. 그 드럼 연주자는 박자를 놓친 적이 없다.

112	**flat** [flæt]	형 평평한, 잔잔한

• Some people still believe that the Earth is **flat**. 어떤 사람들은 여전히 지구가 평평하다고 믿는다.
• There is no wind, and the sea is ＿＿＿＿＿. 바람이 없어서 바다가 잔잔하다.

113	**mechanic** [məkǽnik]	몡 정비사

• Take the car to a **mechanic** to repair it. 차를 정비사에게 가져가서 수리하세요.
• The ＿＿＿＿＿ is checking the engine of a car. 정비사가 자동차의 엔진을 점검하고 있다.

114	**privacy** [práivəsi]	몡 사생활　　　　private 형 사적인

• We should respect other people's **privacy**. 우리는 다른 사람들의 사생활을 존중해야 한다.
• The new law protects ＿＿＿＿＿. 그 새로운 법은 사생활을 보호해 준다.

115	**silent** [sáilənt]	형 조용한, 고요한　　　　silence 몡 고요함, 정적

• Everyone went **silent** when I appeared. 내가 나타나자 모든 사람들이 조용해졌다.
• The stage became dark and ＿＿＿＿＿. 무대가 깜깜해지고 조용해졌다.

116 volunteer
[vὰləntíər]

(명) 자원봉사자　(동) 자발적으로 하다, 자원봉사하다

- Many **volunteers** gathered to clean up the park. 공원을 청소하러 많은 자원봉사자들이 모였다.
- Who will _____ to put the bell on the cat? 누가 자진해서 고양이 목에 방울을 달까?

117 bullet
[búlit]

(명) 총알

- There are some **bullet** holes in the wall. 벽에 몇 군데의 총알 자국이 있다.
- The man was hit by a _____ and died. 그 남자는 총알을 맞고 사망했다.

118 ignore
[ignɔ́ːr]

(동) 무시하다, 모르는 체하다

- At first, most people **ignored** Galileo's findings.
  처음에는 대부분의 사람들이 갈릴레오의 발견을 무시했다.
- Heather _____d her mom's advice. Heather는 엄마의 조언을 듣지 않았다.

119 quality
[kwάləti]

(명) 품질, (사람의) 자질　(형) 품질이 우수한

- Simon has enough **qualities** to be a leader. Simon은 리더가 될 충분한 자질을 갖추고 있다.
- The store sells _____ products. 그 가게는 품질이 우수한 제품을 판매한다.

120 vehicle
[víːikl]

(명) 차량, 탈것

- You must not park your **vehicle** here. 여기에 차량을 주차하면 안 됩니다.
- There are always many _____s on that road. 저 도로에는 항상 많은 차량들이 있다.

Check Up

정답 p.114

A 다음 영어단어를 듣고 해당 번호를 쓰시오. 그 다음, 빈칸에 우리말을 쓰시오. 🎧 20

bullet ☐	degree ☐	volunteer ☐	quality ☐
_____	_____	_____	_____
mechanic ☐	privacy ☐	vehicle ☐	rhythm ☐
_____	_____	_____	_____

B 다음 우리말에 해당하는 영어단어를 쓰시오.

1 무시하다 _____　　2 막대기 _____

3 조용한 _____　　4 평평한 _____

5 소유하다 _____　　6 공격하다 _____

7 (경기 등에서) 이기다 _____

Review

Lesson 7 & Lesson 8

A 다음 영어단어의 우리말을 쓰시오.

1 arrow _____ 2 spend _____

3 pollution _____ 4 silent _____

5 prepare _____ 6 mechanic _____

7 flat _____ 8 bother _____

9 bark _____ 10 ignore _____

11 volunteer _____ 12 pond _____

B 우리말과 일치하도록 알맞은 영어단어를 써넣어 문장을 완성하시오.

1 I like _____ activities like trekking. 나는 트레킹과 같은 야외 활동을 좋아한다.

2 The temperature this morning is 17 _____ s. 오늘 아침 기온은 17도이다.

3 Joshua loves _____ movies about ghosts. Joshua는 귀신이 나오는 공포 영화를 좋아한다.

4 You must not park your _____ here. 여기에 차량을 주차하면 안 됩니다.

5 Who is the _____ of your city? 당신이 사는 도시의 시장은 누구인가요?

6 What's the _____ of your visit? 당신의 방문 목적은 무엇인가요?

7 A lion is _____ ing zebras. 사자 한 마리가 얼룩말들을 공격하고 있다.

8 I arrived at school earlier than _____. 나는 평소보다 일찍 학교에 도착했다.

9 Everyone has his or her _____ personality. 모든 사람은 자신만의 성격을 가지고 있다.

10 I just saw a _____ of lightning. 나는 방금 번개가 번쩍이는 것을 보았다.

C 다음 영어문장이 우리말과 일치하면 O, 그렇지 않으면 X를 쓰시오.

1 The chef stuck the knife into the pumpkin. 요리사는 호박에 칼을 찔러 넣었다. (   )

2 Please turn up the quality on the TV. TV 볼륨을 높여 주세요. (   )

3 I didn't get any reply from Chelsea. 나는 Chelsea에게서 어떤 대답도 듣지 못했다. (   )

4 The new law protects privacy. 그 새로운 법은 사생활을 보호해 준다. (   )

5 The drummer never misses a bullet. 그 드럼 연주자는 박자를 놓친 적이 없다. (   )

D 다음 문장을 듣고 문장을 완성한 후, 빈칸에 쓴 영어단어의 우리말을 쓰시오. 🎧21

1 Some people still believe that the Earth is _____. ➡ ....

2 A young general led the _____ on the town. ➡ ....

3 The radio _____ was too loud. ➡ ....

4 The old man uses a _____ to walk. ➡ ....

5 I cried out in _____ when I saw the monster. ➡ ....

6 Mr. Green has a _____ in physics. ➡ ....

7 I'll go to Canada for the _____ of studying English. ➡ ....

8 The resort has two _____ swimming pools. ➡ ....

9 Who _____s the tallest building in the country? ➡ ....

10 There were many frogs in the _____. ➡ ....

11 Don't _____ to pick me up at the airport. ➡ ....

12 It is not _____ for me to eat so much. ➡ ....

13 The man _____ the weekend watching TV. ➡ ....

14 Take the car to a _____ to repair it. ➡ ....

15 The song starts with a slow _____. ➡ ....

16 Who will _____ to put the bell on the cat? ➡ ....

17 The citizens elected Ms. Hudson _____. ➡ ....

18 My dog only _____s at strangers. ➡ ....

19 There are some _____ holes in the wall. ➡ ....

20 The sunlight was _____ing on the water. ➡ ....

21 Heather _____d her mom's advice. ➡ ....

22 My mom _____d meals for us. ➡ ....

23 The store sells _____ products. ➡ ....

24 There are always many _____s on that road. ➡ ....

25 You must _____ to the letter right now. ➡ ....

26 The stage became dark and _____. ➡ ....

27 Air _____ is a serious problem in China. ➡ ....

28 We should respect other people's _____. ➡ ....

29 Archers fight with bows and _____s. ➡ ....

30 Nicole _____ me in the race. ➡ ....

121	**drawer** [drɔːr]	명 서랍

- My desk **drawers** are full of school supplies. 내 책상 서랍은 학용품으로 가득하다.
- The man took a blue tie out of the _____. 그 남자는 서랍에서 파란 넥타이를 꺼냈다.

122	**bin** [bin]	명 통, 쓰레기통

- I threw the socks into the laundry **bin**. 나는 양말들을 빨래 바구니에 던져 넣었다.
- Put the glass bottles into the recycling _____. 유리병들을 재활용 통에 넣으세요.

123	**still** [stil]	부 여전히, 아직도

- It rained a lot, but it was **still** hot. 많은 비가 내렸지만 여전히 더웠다.
- I _____ remember my first day at elementary school.
 나는 초등학교에서의 첫 날을 아직 기억한다.

124	**rule** [ruːl]	명 규칙

- The **rules** of the new game are easy to understand. 새 게임의 규칙은 이해하기 쉽다.
- You must not break the _____s. 너는 규칙을 어겨서는 안 된다.

125	**role** [roul]	명 역할, 배역

- Alex plays an important **role** in our club. Alex는 우리 동아리에서 중요한 역할을 하고 있다.
- Who will play the _____ of the prince? 누가 왕자 배역을 맡을 거니?

126	**blank** [blæŋk]	형 빈, 비어 있는 명 빈칸

- The teacher gave out **blank** sheets of paper. 그 교사는 빈 종이들을 나누어 주었다.
- Fill in the _____s with your name and address. 빈칸에 이름과 주소를 기입하세요.

127	**float** [flout]	동 (물 위·공기 중에) 떠다니다, (가라앉지 않고) 물에 뜨다

- A balloon is **floating** in the sky. 풍선 하나가 하늘을 떠다니고 있다.
- A stone does not _____ in the water. 돌은 물에 뜨지 않는다.

128	**melt** [melt]	동 녹다

- Ice **melts** when you heat it. 얼음은 열을 가하면 녹는다.
- Chocolate was _____ing in my fingers. 초콜릿이 내 손 안에서 녹고 있었다.

129	**process** [práses]	명 과정, 절차 동 처리하다

- The **process** of building a ship is very complex. 배를 만드는 과정은 매우 복잡하다.
- Your order will be _____ed quickly. 귀하의 주문은 곧 처리될 것입니다.

130	**slide** [slaid] slide-slid-slid	동 미끄러지다 명 미끄럼틀

- Some children are **sliding** on the ice. 몇몇 아이들이 얼음 위에서 미끄럼을 타고 있다.
- This swimming pool has water _____s. 이 수영장에는 워터 슬라이드가 있다.

131 vote
[vout]

동 투표하다   명 (선거에서의) 표, 투표

- My sister didn't **vote** in the last election. 우리 누나는 지난 선거에서 투표를 하지 않았다.
- How many _____s did the new class president get?
  새로 반장이 된 학생은 몇 표를 받았니?

132 bully
[búli]

동 약자를 괴롭히다, 따돌리다   명 약자를 괴롭히는 사람

- Ethan is being **bullied** by his classmates. Ethan은 반 친구들에게 괴롭힘을 당하고 있다.
- Jenny used to be the school _____. Jenny는 한때 학교에서 친구들을 괴롭히는 아이였다.

133 imagine
[imǽdʒin]

동 상상하다   imagination 명 상상

- I can't **imagine** a world without the Internet. 나는 인터넷이 없는 세상은 상상할 수 없어.
- George never _____d meeting his mom there.
  George는 그곳에서 엄마를 만나리라고는 상상조차 하지 못했다.

134 rather
[rǽðər]

부 상당히, 꽤

- That is a **rather** difficult question for me. 그것은 나에게 상당히 어려운 질문이다.
- The movie was _____ long and boring. 그 영화는 꽤 길고 지루했다.

135 warn
[wɔ:rn]

동 위험을 알리다/미리 주의를 주다, 경고하다

- The sign **warned** us of the steep stairs. 그 표지판은 가파른 계단에 대한 주의를 주었다.
- The teacher _____ed me not to be late again.
  선생님은 나에게 다시는 늦지 말라고 경고하셨다.

Check Up

정답 p.115

A 다음 영어단어를 듣고 해당 번호를 쓰시오. 그 다음, 빈칸에 우리말을 쓰시오. 🎧23

slide	☐	bin	☐	blank	☐	rather	☐
_____		_____		_____		_____	
bully	☐	imagine	☐	warn	☐	float	☐
_____		_____		_____		_____	

B 다음 우리말에 해당하는 영어단어를 쓰시오.

1 여전히 _____
2 서랍 _____
3 규칙 _____
4 투표하다 _____
5 녹다 _____
6 과정 _____
7 역할 _____

33

136	**ease** [iːz]	몡 쉬움, 편안함	easy 혱 쉬운

• Tyler solved the math questions with **ease**. Tyler는 수학 문제들을 쉽게 풀었다.
• I cannot feel at _____ among strangers. 나는 낯선 사람들과 함께 있으면 편하지가 않다.

---

137 **past**
[pæst]

혱 지나간, 이전의   몡 과거

• My dad sometimes tells me about his **past** experiences.
아빠는 가끔 자신의 과거 경험을 나에게 이야기해 주신다.
• I think people were happier in the _____. 나는 사람들이 과거에 더 행복했다고 생각한다.

---

138 **storm**
[stɔːrm]

몡 폭풍

• Lots of tall trees fell down in the **storm**. 폭풍으로 인해 키 큰 나무들이 많이 쓰러졌다.
• Because of the _____, we couldn't go out. 폭풍 때문에 우리는 외출할 수 없었다.

---

139 **a bit**
[ə bit]

조금, 약간

• Julia moved **a bit** closer to me. Julia가 내 쪽으로 조금 더 가까이 왔다.
• My brother is _____ taller than me. 우리 형은 나보다 조금 더 크다.

---

140 **plate**
[pleit]

몡 접시

• My mom put a piece of cake on my **plate**. 엄마는 내 접시에 케이크 한 조각을 놓으셨다.
• The _____s are dirty. I'll wash them. 접시들이 더럽네. 내가 설거지 할게.

---

141 **blind**
[blaind]

혱 눈이 보이지 않는, 시각 장애의   몡 블라인드

• These are guide dogs for **blind** people. 이 개들은 시각 장애인 안내견이다.
• I opened the _____s to look out the window. 나는 블라인드를 올려서 창밖을 보았다.

---

142 **forecast**
[fɔ́ːrkæ̀st]

몡 예측, 예보   동 예측하다

• The weather **forecast** says it will snow tomorrow. 일기 예보에 따르면 내일은 눈이 올 것이다.
• The report _____s an economic growth. 그 보고서는 경제 성장을 예측하고 있다.

---

143 **mental**
[méntəl]

혱 정신적인

• The patient has some **mental** problems. 그 환자는 정신적인 문제를 겪고 있다.
• Does food affect _____ health? 음식이 정신적인 건강에 영향을 미칠까?

---

144 **produce**
[prədjúːs]

동 생산하다, 만들다   production 몡 생산

• The factory **produces** about 1,000 cars a day. 그 공장은 하루에 1,000여 대의 자동차를 만든다.
• Most wool is _____ed in Australia. 대부분의 울은 호주에서 생산된다.

---

145 **society**
[səsáiəti]

몡 사회

• I want big changes in our **society**. 나는 우리 사회에서 큰 변화가 일어나기를 바란다.
• Stress is a major problem in our _____. 스트레스는 우리 사회의 큰 문제이다.

146

weigh
[wei]

동 무게가 ~이다, 무게를 재다

weight 명무게

- The big dog **weighs** over 12kg. 그 커다란 개는 무게가 12kg 이상 나간다.
- The airline will ⬚⬚⬚⬚⬚ your luggage. 항공사는 당신의 수화물 무게를 잴 것이다.

147

pretend
[priténd]

동 ~인 척하다

- Don't **pretend** to know everything. 모든 것을 아는 척하지 마시오.
- I ⬚⬚⬚⬚ed I was sleeping when Dad called me.
  아빠가 부르셨을 때 나는 잠을 자고 있는 척 했다.

148

include
[inklú:d]

동 포함하다, 포함시키다

- Shakespeare's works **include** *Romeo and Juliet* and *Hamlet*.
  셰익스피어의 작품 중에는 '로미오와 줄리엣'과 '햄릿'이 있다.
- Please ⬚⬚⬚⬚⬚ my name on the waiting list. 대기자 명단에 제 이름을 넣어 주세요.

149

realize
[rí(:)əlàiz]

동 깨닫다, 알아차리다

- Ian **realized** that he made a big mistake. Ian은 자신이 큰 실수를 했다는 것을 깨달았다.
- I ⬚⬚⬚⬚d how important friends are. 나는 친구가 얼마나 중요한지 깨달았다.

150

whole
[houl]

형 전체의

- We spent the **whole** day fishing at the lake. 우리는 호수에서 낚시를 하며 하루를 보냈다.
- The little boy ate the ⬚⬚⬚⬚ pizza by himself.
  그 어린 남자아이는 혼자서 피자를 다 먹었다.

Check Up

정답 p.115

A 다음 영어단어를 듣고 해당 번호를 쓰시오. 그 다음, 빈칸에 우리말을 쓰시오. 🎧25

realize ☐	weigh ☐	pretend ☐	forecast ☐
_____	_____	_____	_____
society ☐	blind ☐	past ☐	a bit ☐
_____	_____	_____	_____

B 다음 우리말에 해당하는 영어단어를 쓰시오.

1 쉬움 _____

2 접시 _____

3 정신적인 _____

4 생산하다 _____

5 포함하다 _____

6 폭풍 _____

7 전체의 _____

A 다음 영어단어의 우리말을 쓰시오.

1 past _____   2 society _____

3 blank _____   4 imagine _____

5 realize _____   6 pretend _____

7 storm _____   8 whole _____

9 a bit _____   10 melt _____

11 blind _____   12 drawer _____

B 우리말과 일치하도록 알맞은 영어단어를 써넣어 문장을 완성하시오.

1 It rained a lot, but it was _____ hot. 많은 비가 내렸지만 여전히 더웠다.

2 The patient has some _____ problems. 그 환자는 정신적인 문제를 겪고 있다.

3 The _____s are dirty. I'll wash them. 접시들이 더럽네. 내가 설거지 할게.

4 The _____ of building a ship is very complex. 배를 만드는 과정은 매우 복잡하다.

5 My sister didn't _____ in the last election. 우리 누나는 지난 선거에서 투표를 하지 않았다.

6 Who will play the _____ of the prince? 누가 왕자 역할을 맡을 거니?

7 That is a _____ difficult question for me. 그것은 나에게 상당히 어려운 질문이다.

8 The _____s of the new game are easy to understand. 새 게임의 규칙은 이해하기 쉽다.

9 A balloon is _____ing in the sky. 풍선 하나가 하늘을 떠다니고 있다.

10 The big dog _____s over 12kg. 그 커다란 개는 무게가 12kg 이상 나간다.

C 다음 영어문장이 우리말과 일치하면 O, 그렇지 않으면 X를 쓰시오.

1 The factory produces about 1,000 cars a day. 그 공장은 하루에 1,000여 대의 자동차를 만든다. (   )

2 Please include my name on the waiting list. 대기자 명단에 제 이름을 넣어 주세요. (   )

3 The weather bin says it will snow tomorrow. 일기 예보에 따르면 내일은 눈이 올 것이다. (   )

4 Tyler solved the math questions with ease. Tyler는 수학 문제들을 쉽게 풀었다. (   )

5 Some children are sliding on the ice. 몇몇 아이들이 얼음 위에서 미끄럼을 타고 있다. (   )

D 다음 문장을 듣고 문장을 완성한 후, 빈칸에 쓴 영어단어의 우리말을 쓰시오. 🎧26

1 I threw the socks into the laundry _____. ➡ ....

2 Alex plays an important _____ in our club. ➡ ....

3 I can't _____ a world without the Internet. ➡ ....

4 The sign _____ed us of the steep stairs. ➡ ....

5 Fill in the _____s with your name and address. ➡ ....

6 I cannot feel at _____ among strangers. ➡ ....

7 The movie was _____ long and boring. ➡ ....

8 Does food affect _____ health? ➡ ....

9 Ian _____d that he made a big mistake. ➡ ....

10 My desk _____s are full of school supplies. ➡ ....

11 I think people were happier in the _____. ➡ ....

12 A stone does not _____ in the water. ➡ ....

13 Most wool is _____ed in Australia. ➡ ....

14 Lots of tall trees fell down in the _____. ➡ ....

15 You must not break the _____s. ➡ ....

16 Julia moved _____ closer to me. ➡ ....

17 The airline will _____ your luggage. ➡ ....

18 How many _____s did the new class president get? ➡ ....

19 Ice _____s when you heat it. ➡ ....

20 My mom put a piece of cake on my _____. ➡ ....

21 Your order will be _____ed quickly. ➡ ....

22 Jenny used to be the school _____. ➡ ....

23 This swimming pool has water _____s. ➡ ....

24 I opened the _____s to look out the window. ➡ ....

25 Stress is a major problem in our _____. ➡ ....

26 Don't _____ to know everything. ➡ ....

27 Shakespeare's works _____ *Romeo and Juliet* and *Hamlet*. ➡ ....

28 The little boy ate the _____ pizza by himself. ➡ ....

29 The report _____s an economic growth. ➡ ....

30 I _____ remember my first day at elementary school. ➡ ....

Ⓐ 영어단어는 우리말로, 우리말은 영어단어로 바꿔 쓰시오.

1 among	➔	26 비록 ~이지만	➔
2 trouble	➔	27 뱀	➔
3 physical	➔	28 행진	➔
4 plus	➔	29 밤 12시	➔
5 experience	➔	30 새 둥지	➔
6 shade	➔	31 환경	➔
7 thief	➔	32 가장 중요한	➔
8 goods	➔	33 주인	➔
9 pair	➔	34 독특한	➔
10 billion	➔	35 손잡이	➔
11 award	➔	36 (숫자의 합을) 세다	➔
12 blossom	➔	37 발생하다	➔
13 argue	➔	38 연못	➔
14 balance	➔	39 (시간·돈을) 쓰다	➔
15 mental	➔	40 소유하다	➔
16 society	➔	41 차량	➔
17 few	➔	42 규칙	➔
18 border	➔	43 비어 있는	➔
19 reply	➔	44 이상한	➔
20 treasure	➔	45 바람이 불다	➔
21 grab	➔	46 자리, 자세	➔
22 envelope	➔	47 행동, 행위	➔
23 beg	➔	48 위험을 알리다	➔
24 pole	➔	49 흔들다	➔
25 shoulder	➔	50 현명한	➔

B 우리말과 일치하도록 알맞은 영어단어를 써넣어 문장을 완성하시오.

1 Be sure to _____ the answer on the exam sheet. 잊지 말고 시험지에 답을 <u>표시해</u>.

2 We left early to _____ traffic jams. 교통 체증을 <u>피하기 위해</u> 우리는 일찍 나섰다.

3 That doesn't _____ now. 그것이 지금 <u>문제가 되지는</u> 않아.

4 It's _____ cold today. 오늘은 <u>꽤</u> 춥다.

5 Robert is much more _____ than I am. Robert는 나보다 훨씬 더 <u>활동적이다</u>.

6 I have a sore throat so I can't _____. 목이 따가워서 잘 <u>삼키지</u> 못하겠어.

7 The puzzle is _____ for me to solve. 그 퍼즐은 내가 풀기에 <u>간단했다</u>.

8 I _____ed when the band appeared. 그 밴드가 등장했을 때 나는 <u>소리를 질렀다</u>.

9 A note was _____ed on the door. 문에 쪽지 한 장이 <u>붙어 있었다</u>.

10 The baseball game was _____ed because of rain. 비 때문에 야구 경기가 <u>취소되었다</u>.

11 I'll bring the tent. Can you _____ the food? 내가 텐트를 갖고 올게. 너는 음식을 <u>준비할래</u>?

12 My _____ in life is to serve others. 나의 인생 <u>목표는</u> 타인을 위해 봉사하는 것이다.

13 _____ out your tongue and say "Aah." 혀를 <u>내밀고</u> "아" 하고 말하세요.

14 I like his _____ of speaking. 나는 그가 말하는 <u>방식이</u> 마음에 든다.

15 The candy was in the egg _____. 그 사탕은 계란 <u>모양이었다</u>.

16 I _____ed the invitation to the party. 나는 파티 초대를 <u>수락했다</u>.

17 I made a _____. The correct number is four. 내가 <u>실수를</u> 했어. 정답은 4야.

18 Amy and Jessica _____ an apartment. Amy와 Jessica는 아파트에 <u>같이 산다</u>.

19 Put the chairs on the _____ ground. 그 의자들을 <u>평평한</u> 땅 위에 놓으세요.

20 Sarah was _____d for her volunteer work. Sarah는 자원봉사로 <u>칭찬을 받았다</u>.

21 Jake annoys me, so I just _____ him. Jake가 나를 귀찮게 해서 나는 그냥 걔를 <u>무시한다</u>.

22 We are going to _____ on the beach. 우리는 해변에서 <u>휴식을 취할</u> 것이다.

23 This is a high _____ suit. 이것은 <u>고품질의</u> 정장이다.

24 Brad paid the _____ amount. Brad가 <u>전체</u> 금액을 지불했다.

25 Don't go to the movie theater _____ me. 나 <u>없이</u> 극장에 가지 마.

C 다음 문장에 들어갈 알맞은 단어를 고르시오.

1 Global warming is a [wise / serious / physical] matter.

2 What's the [price / rhythm / degree] of the concert ticket?

3 I heard somebody [ignoring / explaining / shouting] my name.

4 Is it [strange / possible / polite] to buy the book online?

5 Karen is the [president / mechanic / mayor] of our book club.

6 What's the [trouble / process / purpose] of your visit?

7 My sister didn't [vote / stick / forecast] in the last election.

8 The [volumes / pollutions / plates] are dirty. I'll wash them.

9 These are guide dogs for [total / asleep / blind] people.

10 I'd like to [shake / order / announce] a pepperoni pizza.

11 We used [pan / envelope / mud] to make pottery.

12 Which do you [imagine / prefer / mark], coffee or tea?

13 It rained a lot, but it was [still / maybe / fortunately] hot.

14 I burned my [tongue / item / position] on the hot soup.

15 The bug is not dead. It's [total / unique / alive].

16 Kevin plays cello in the school [master / orchestra / volunteer].

17 Ice [slides / floats / melts] when you heat it.

18 It is not [simple / polite / strange] to whisper in front of others.

19 The factory [weights / produces / warns] about 1,000 cars a day.

20 Please [own / experience / include] my name on the waiting list.

21 The mom was [gentle / upset / total] when her son spilled the milk again.

22 Can I ask you a [role / bullet / favor]?

23 A [few / typical / tough] Korean meal includes rice, soup, and side dishes.

24 The drought did great [storm / harm / flash] to the crops.

25 Don't [bother / trust / pretend] to pick me up at the airport.

D 다음 단어의 바뀐 품사를 보기 에서 찾아 빈칸에 쓰고, 그 단어의 우리말을 쓰시오.

보기 seriously imagination announcement announcement weight noisy
private fortunate production production shiny ability
pollute horrible silence silence easy usually

1 (형) serious → (부) _____ ➡ ....

2 (부) fortunately → (형) _____ ➡ ....

3 (명) noise → (형) _____ ➡ ....

4 (형) able → (명) _____ ➡ ....

5 (동) announce → (명) _____ ➡ ....

6 (명) pollution → (동) _____ ➡ ....

7 (동) shine → (형) _____ ➡ ....

8 (명) horror → (형) _____ ➡ ....

9 (형) usual → (부) _____ ➡ ....

10 (명) privacy → (형) _____ ➡ ....

11 (형) silent → (명) _____ ➡ ....

12 (동) imagine → (명) _____ ➡ ....

13 (명) ease → (형) _____ ➡ ....

14 (동) produce → (명) _____ ➡ ....

15 (동) weigh → (명) _____ ➡ ....

➕ TIP

영어에는 동사를 명사로 만드는 다양한 접미사가 있는데, 그 중 대표적인 접미사는 –ion/ation입니다. 동사와 –ion/ation이 결합하여 명사로 바뀌는 예를 알아볼까요?

☆ pollute (오염시키다) + ion = pollution (오염) ☆ produce (생산하다) + ation = production (생산)
☆ imagine (상상하다) + ation = imagination (상상) ☆ explain (설명하다) + ation = explanation (설명)

151	**hole** [houl]	몡 구멍

- Moles live in **holes** in the ground. 두더지는 땅굴에서 산다.
- Your right sock has a ⬜⬜⬜ in the back. 네 오른쪽 양말 뒤쪽에 구멍이 나 있어.

152	**pattern** [pǽtərn]	몡 무늬, (정형화된) 패턴/양식

- The dress has a floral **pattern**. 그 드레스는 꽃무늬가 있다.
- You should keep healthy sleep ⬜⬜⬜s. 너는 건강에 좋은 수면 패턴을 가져야 한다.

153	**sore** [sɔːr]	혱 아픈, 따가운

- I have a **sore** throat with the flu. 나는 독감으로 목이 아파.
- After climbing the mountain, my legs got ⬜⬜⬜. 등산을 한 후 나는 다리가 아팠다.

154	**blanket** [blǽŋkit]	몡 담요, 이불

- There is no **blanket** on the bed. 침대에 이불이 없다.
- This ⬜⬜⬜ will keep you warm. 이 담요가 네 몸을 따뜻하게 해 줄 거야.

155	**sense** [sens]	몡 감각 동 감지하다, 느끼다

- Taste is one of the five **senses**. 미각은 오감 중 하나이다.
- I ⬜⬜⬜d my mom was hiding something. 나는 엄마가 무언가를 감추고 있다고 느꼈다.

156	**breathe** [briːð]	동 숨쉬다, 호흡하다 breath 몡 호흡

- All animals need air to **breathe**. 모든 동물들은 호흡하기 위해 공기가 필요하다.
- This room is full of smoke. I can't ⬜⬜⬜ here.
  이 방은 연기로 가득해. 숨을 쉴 수가 없어.

157	**forgive** [fərgív] forgive-forgave-forgiven	동 용서하다

- Kevin apologized, but I didn't **forgive** him. Kevin이 사과했지만, 나는 그를 용서하지 않았다.
- My mom ⬜⬜⬜ me for telling a lie. 엄마는 내가 거짓말한 것을 용서해 주셨다.

158	**million** [míljən]	몡 백만

- Gwangju has around 1.5 **million** people. 광주의 인구는 약 150만 명이다.
- Who donated six ⬜⬜⬜ dollars to the library? 누가 그 도서관에 6백만 달러를 기부했니?

159	**punish** [pʌ́niʃ]	동 (잘못된 행위에 대한) 벌을 주다

- I was **punished** for fighting with my brother. 나는 동생과 싸워서 벌을 받았다.
- Why did the teacher ⬜⬜⬜ Mia? 선생님은 왜 Mia에게 벌을 주셨니?

160	**grade** [greid]	몡 등급/점수, 학년

- Lily got a poor **grade** on the math exam. Lily는 수학 시험에서 낮은 점수를 받았다.
- My youngest brother is in fourth ⬜⬜⬜. 내 막내 동생은 4학년이다.

161 wheel
[hwi:l]

몡 (자동차의) 바퀴, 핸들

- Most vehicles have two or four **wheels**. 대부분의 교통 수단은 바퀴가 두 개이거나 네 개이다.
- The driver suddenly turned the   . 운전자는 갑자기 핸들을 돌렸다.

162 capital
[kǽpitəl]

몡 (나라의) 수도   혱 대문자의

- The **capital** of Vietnam is Hanoi. 베트남의 수도는 하노이이다.
- Please write your name in   letters. 이름을 대문자로 적으세요.

163 increase
[inkrí:s]

통 증가하다   몡 증가 [ínkri:s]

- The population of our country is **increasing**. 우리나라의 인구는 증가하고 있다.
- Nobody wants a tax   . 아무도 세금 인상을 원하지 않는다.

164 recognize
[rékəgnàiz]

통 알아보다, 인식하다

- The actor wore sunglasses, so no one **recognized** him.
  그 배우는 선글라스를 쓰고 있어서, 아무도 그를 알아보지 못했다.
- I   d my mistake and corrected it. 나는 실수한 곳을 찾아내어 바르게 고쳤다.

165 humid
[hjú:mid]

혱 (날씨가) 습한

- Indonesia is hot and **humid** most of the year. 인도네시아는 연중 덥고 습하다.
- People feel uncomfortable in   weather.
  사람들은 날씨가 습할 때 불쾌감을 느낀다.

Check Up

정답 p.117

A 다음 영어단어를 듣고 해당 번호를 쓰시오. 그 다음, 빈칸에 우리말을 쓰시오. 🎧28

blanket ☐	sore ☐	grade ☐	breathe ☐
_____	_____	_____	_____

recognize ☐	increase ☐	punish ☐	forgive ☐
_____	_____	_____	_____

B 다음 우리말에 해당하는 영어단어를 쓰시오.

1 구멍   _____   2 감각   _____

3 (자동차의) 바퀴   _____   4 습한   _____

5 무늬   _____   6 (나라의) 수도   _____

7 백만   _____

Lesson 12

166 fair
[fɛ́ər]

형 공정한   명 박람회

- All of us want to play a **fair** game. 우리 모두는 공정한 경기를 원한다.
- The world's largest book ⬜⬜⬜ is held in Frankfurt.
  세계에서 가장 큰 도서전은 프랑크푸르트에서 열린다.

167 pepper
[pépər]

명 후추

- Add a little salt and **pepper** to the steak. 스테이크에 약간의 소금과 후추를 뿌리세요.
- I'm allergic to black ⬜⬜⬜. 나는 검은 후추에 알레르기가 있다.

168 stretch
[stretʃ]

동 (길이·폭 등을) 늘이다, 뻗다

- **Stretch** your arms and legs before you exercise. 운동을 하기 전에 팔과 다리를 쭉 뻗으세요.
- The baby ⬜⬜⬜ed out his hand to take the cup. 그 아기는 손을 뻗어서 컵을 집었다.

169 cave
[keiv]

명 동굴

- Many bats live in the **cave**. 그 동굴에는 많은 박쥐들이 살고 있다.
- The explorer went deeper into the ⬜⬜⬜. 그 탐험가는 동굴의 더 안쪽으로 들어갔다.

170 sheet
[ʃiːt]

명 침대에 까는 천/시트, 종이 한 장

- I change the **sheets** on my bed once a week. 나는 일주일에 한 번 침대의 시트를 간다.
- Please give me a ⬜⬜⬜ of paper. 종이 한 장을 주세요.

171 bride
[braid]

명 신부

- Why does a **bride** wear a white wedding dress? 신부는 왜 하얀색 웨딩드레스를 입을까?
- The ⬜⬜⬜ and groom look very happy. 그 신랑과 신부는 매우 행복해 보인다.

172 fortune
[fɔ́ːrtʃən]

명 (많은 돈의) 재산, 운   fortunate 형 운이 좋은

- The rich man left a large **fortune** to his son. 그 부자는 아들에게 많은 재산을 남겼다.
- Adam had the good ⬜⬜⬜ to win a lottery. Adam은 복권에 당첨되는 행운이 있었다.

173 miracle
[mírəkl]

명 기적

- It is a **miracle** that no one was injured in the fire. 화재에서 아무도 다치지 않은 것은 기적이다.
- I believe that ⬜⬜⬜s often happen. 나는 종종 기적이 일어난다고 믿는다.

174 pure
[pjuər]

형 다른 것이 섞이지 않은, 순수한

- Is the medal made of **pure** gold? 그 메달은 순금으로 만들어졌나요?
- The orange juice is 100% ⬜⬜⬜. 그 오렌지 주스는 100% 오렌지 과즙이다.

175 spoil
[spɔil]

동 망치다, 못쓰게 만들다

- The heavy rain **spoiled** our picnic. 폭우 때문에 우리의 소풍은 망쳤다.
- Kelly ate ⬜⬜⬜ed food and got sick. Kelly는 상한 음식을 먹고 아팠다.

176 wonder
[wʌ́ndər]

⟨동⟩ 궁금해하다
- I **wonder** why Jake didn't come to school today. 나는 Jake가 왜 오늘 결석했는지 궁금하다.
- I _____ who will win the next World Cup.
  나는 다음 월드컵 경기에서 누가 우승할지 궁금하다.

177 chase
[tʃeis]

⟨동⟩ 쫓다, 추격하다
- A cat is **chasing** after a mouse. 고양이가 쥐를 쫓고 있다.
- A police officer _____ d the thief and caught him.
  한 경찰관이 도둑을 추격하여 그를 잡았다.

178 intelligent
[intélidʒənt]

⟨형⟩ 지능이 높은, 똑똑한   intelligence ⟨명⟩ 지능
- Humans are more **intelligent** than other animals. 인간은 다른 동물들보다 지능이 높다.
- Paige is _____, but she doesn't like studying.
  Paige는 똑똑하지만 공부를 좋아하지는 않는다.

179 regular
[régjələr]

⟨형⟩ 정기적인/규칙적인, 횟수가 잦은
- The music festival became a **regular** event. 그 음악 축제는 정기적인 행사가 되었다.
- Ms. Wilson is one of the store's _____ customers.
  Wilson 씨는 그 가게의 단골 고객 중 하나이다.

180 underground
[ʌ̀ndərgráund]

⟨형⟩ 지하의   ⟨부⟩ 지하에
- Many trains travel through the **underground** tunnel. 많은 기차가 지하 터널을 지나간다.
- The treasure is hidden somewhere _____. 그 보물은 지하 어딘가에 숨겨져 있다.

Check Up

정답 p.117

A 다음 영어단어를 듣고 해당 번호를 쓰시오. 그 다음, 빈칸에 우리말을 쓰시오. 🎧30

intelligent ☐	miracle ☐	spoil ☐	stretch ☐
_____	_____	_____	_____

underground ☐	pepper ☐	fortune ☐	sheet ☐
_____	_____	_____	_____

B 다음 우리말에 해당하는 영어단어를 쓰시오.

1 순수한   _____   2 공정한   _____

3 궁금해하다   _____   4 동굴   _____

5 정기적인   _____   6 신부   _____

7 쫓다   _____

정답 p.117

A 다음 영어단어의 우리말을 쓰시오.

1 million _____   2 spoil _____

3 miracle _____   4 sore _____

5 recognize _____   6 chase _____

7 intelligent _____   8 increase _____

9 sense _____   10 wonder _____

11 pure _____   12 fortune _____

B 우리말과 일치하도록 알맞은 영어단어를 써넣어 문장을 완성하시오.

1 Many bats live in the _____. 그 동굴에는 많은 박쥐들이 살고 있다.

2 I'm allergic to black _____. 나는 검은 후추에 알레르기가 있다.

3 Moles live in _____s in the ground. 두더지는 땅굴에서 산다.

4 The _____ of Vietnam is Hanoi. 베트남의 수도는 하노이이다.

5 Why does a _____ wear a white wedding dress? 신부는 왜 하얀색 웨딩드레스를 입을까?

6 Indonesia is hot and _____ most of the year. 인도네시아는 연중 덥고 습하다.

7 All animals need air to _____. 모든 동물들은 호흡하기 위해 공기가 필요하다

8 All of us want to play a _____ game. 우리 모두는 공정한 경기를 원한다.

9 Lily got a poor _____ on the math exam. Lily는 수학 시험에서 낮은 점수를 받았다.

10 The music festival became a _____ event. 그 음악 축제는 정기적인 행사가 되었다.

C 다음 영어문장이 우리말과 일치하면 O, 그렇지 않으면 X를 쓰시오.

1 The dress has a floral pattern. 그 드레스는 꽃무늬가 있다. ( )

2 My mom punished me for telling a lie. 엄마는 내가 거짓말한 것을 용서해 주셨다. ( )

3 Stretch your arms and legs before you exercise. 운동을 하기 전에 팔과 다리를 쭉 뻗으세요. ( )

4 Many trains travel through the underground tunnel. 많은 기차가 지하 터널을 지나간다. ( )

5 There is no wheel on the bed. 침대에 이불이 없다. ( )

D 다음 문장을 듣고 문장을 완성한 후, 빈칸에 쓴 영어단어의 우리말을 쓰시오. 🎧31

1 Gwangju has around 1.5 _____ people. ➜ ....

2 The explorer went deeper into the _____. ➜ ....

3 My youngest brother is in fourth _____. ➜ ....

4 I _____d my mistake and corrected it. ➜ ....

5 Nobody wants a tax _____. ➜ ....

6 I was _____ed for fighting with my brother. ➜ ....

7 The baby _____ed out his hand to take the cup. ➜ ....

8 Most vehicles have two or four _____s. ➜ ....

9 The world's largest book _____ is held in Frankfurt. ➜ ....

10 I have a _____ throat with the flu. ➜ ....

11 I change the _____s on my bed once a week. ➜ ....

12 Add a little salt and _____ to the steak. ➜ ....

13 People feel uncomfortable in _____ weather. ➜ ....

14 Please write your name in _____ letters. ➜ ....

15 This _____ will keep you warm. ➜ ....

16 You should keep healthy sleep _____s. ➜ ....

17 Ms. Wilson is one of the store's _____ customers. ➜ ....

18 The rich man left a large _____ to his son. ➜ ....

19 The heavy rain _____ed our picnic. ➜ ....

20 Kevin apologized, but I didn't _____ him. ➜ ....

21 I believe that _____s often happen. ➜ ....

22 The _____ and groom look very happy. ➜ ....

23 The orange juice is 100% _____. ➜ ....

24 Taste is one of the five _____s ➜ ....

25 I _____ who will win the next World Cup. ➜ ....

26 Humans are more _____ than other animals. ➜ ....

27 A police officer _____d the thief and caught him. ➜ ....

28 The treasure is hidden somewhere _____. ➜ ....

29 This room is full of smoke. I can't _____ here. ➜ ....

30 Your right sock has a _____ in the back. ➜ ....

181 final
[fáinəl]

⟨형⟩ 마지막의, 최종의　　　　　　　　　　　finally ⟨부⟩ 마지막으로, 마침내

- What was the **final** score of today's game? 오늘 경기의 최종 점수는 무엇이었니?
- We have to make the _____ decision now. 우리는 지금 최종 결정을 내려야 해.

182 piece
[pi:s]

⟨명⟩ 조각

- The baseball bat broke into two **pieces**. 야구방망이가 두 조각이 났다.
- I just ate the last _____ of the apple pie. 나는 방금 애플파이의 마지막 조각을 먹었다.

183 such
[sətʃ]

⟨형⟩ 그러한, 그런　　⟨부⟩ 너무나

- Why do you believe **such** things? 너는 왜 그런 것을 믿니?
- It's _____ a beautiful day, isn't it? 너무나 화창한 날이야, 그렇지 않니?

184 chest
[tʃest]

⟨명⟩ 가슴/흉부, 상자

- I have a pain in my **chest**. 나는 가슴에 통증이 있다.
- There were some old letters in the _____. 그 상자에 오래된 편지들이 몇 통 있었다.

185 shower
[ʃáuər]

⟨명⟩ 샤워, 소나기

- I take a **shower** every morning. 나는 아침마다 샤워를 한다.
- I was caught in a _____ on my way home. 나는 집에 가다가 소나기를 만났다.

186 celebrate
[séləbrèit]

⟨동⟩ 축하하다, 기념하다　　　　　　　　　celebration ⟨명⟩ 축하

- Let's **celebrate** our victory! 우리의 승리를 축하합시다!
- Americans _____ their independence on July 4.
  미국인들은 7월 4일에 독립을 기념한다.

187 spirit
[spírit]

⟨명⟩ 정신, 영혼

- Yoga can strengthen your body and **spirit**. 요가는 신체와 정신을 강하게 만들어 줄 수 있다.
- The girl has a pure _____. 그 여자아이는 순수한 영혼을 갖고 있다.

188 monster
[mάnstər]

⟨명⟩ 괴물

- The story is about a big scary **monster**. 그 이야기는 크고 무서운 괴물에 관한 것이다.
- Do you believe that a _____ lives in the lake? 너는 그 호수에 괴물이 살고 있다고 믿니?

189 raise
[reiz]

⟨동⟩ (위로) 들어올리다, (동·식물을) 기르다

- Natalie **raised** her hand and asked a question. Natalie는 손을 들고 질문을 했다.
- Mr. Hill _____s cattle on his farm. Hill 씨는 목장에서 소를 기른다.

190 spread
[spred]
spread-spread-spread

⟨동⟩ 펼치다, 퍼지다/확산되다

- My dad **spread** the carpet on the floor. 아빠는 바닥에 카펫을 까셨다.
- The flu can _____ from person to person. 독감은 사람들을 통해 퍼져 나갈 수 있다.

191 yell
[jel]
(동) 소리를 지르다, 고함치다
- "Stop it!" My sister **yelled** at me. "그만 해!"라고 언니가 나에게 소리를 질렀다.
- My mom never _____s although she sometimes gets angry.
  엄마는 화가 나도 절대 고함치지 않으신다.

192 cheek
[tʃiːk]
(명) 볼, 뺨
- The woman kissed her baby on the **cheek**. 그 여자는 아기의 볼에 뽀뽀했다.
- My tears were running down my _____s. 눈물이 내 뺨을 타고 흘러내렸다.

193 invent
[invént]
(동) 발명하다   invention (명) 발명
- The light bulb was **invented** by Thomas Edition. 전구는 토마스 에디슨에 의해 발명되었다.
- Do you know who _____ed the first airplane?
  너는 최초의 비행기를 발명한 사람이 누구인지 아니?

194 remain
[riméin]
(동) 여전히 ~이다, 남아 있다
- Please **remain** seated during the performance. 공연 중에는 자리에 앉아 계십시오.
- Only five minutes _____ in the exam. 시험 시간이 5분 밖에 남지 않았다.

195 survey
[sə́:rvei]
(명) 설문 조사   (동) 설문 조사하다 [sə:rvéi]
- The school took a **survey** of all the students. 그 학교는 전교생을 대상으로 설문 조사를 했다.
- The store _____s its customers every month.
  그 가게는 매달 고객들을 대상으로 설문 조사를 한다.

Check Up
정답 p.117

A 다음 영어단어를 듣고 해당 번호를 쓰시오. 그 다음, 빈칸에 우리말을 쓰시오. 🎧33

| piece | ☐ | shower | ☐ | such | ☐ | yell | ☐ |

_____   _____   _____   _____

| raise | ☐ | spirit | ☐ | celebrate | ☐ | spread | ☐ |

_____   _____   _____   _____

B 다음 우리말에 해당하는 영어단어를 쓰시오.

1 마지막의 _____   2 괴물 _____

3 여전히 ~이다 _____   4 설문 조사 _____

5 볼, 뺨 _____   6 발명하다 _____

7 가슴 _____

196	**flood** [flʌd]	명 홍수 동 (강 등의) 물이 넘치게 하다

- The town was totally destroyed by the **flood**. 홍수로 인해 마을 전체가 파괴되었다.
- The river was _____ed by the heavy rain. 폭우로 강이 범람했다.

197	**fur** [fəːr]	명 털, 모피

- The cat is covered in black **fur**. 그 고양이는 검정색 털로 뒤덮여 있다.
- These coats are made from animal _____. 이 코트들은 동물의 털로 만들어졌다.

198	**sweat** [swet]	동 땀을 흘리다 명 땀

- Some people **sweat** more than others. 어떤 사람들은 다른 사람들보다 땀을 더 많이 흘린다.
- My uniform was wet with _____. 내 유니폼은 땀으로 젖었다.

199	**vacation** [veikéiʃən]	명 휴가, 방학

- They spent their **vacation** in Hawaii. 그들은 하와이에서 휴가를 보냈다.
- We are looking forward to summer _____. 우리는 여름 방학을 기다리고 있다.

200	**silver** [sílvər]	명 은

- In most cases, **silver** is cheaper than gold. 대부분의 경우에 은은 금보다 싸다.
- Amy finished in second place, so she received the _____ medal.
  Amy는 2등을 하여 은메달을 받았다.

201	**challenge** [tʃǽlindʒ]	동 도전하다 명 하기 어려운 일

- Blake **challenged** me to a game of ping pong. Blake가 나에게 탁구를 치자고 도전했다.
- Knitting a muffler is a _____ for me. 머플러를 뜨는 것은 나에게 쉽지 않은 일이다.

202	**greet** [griːt]	동 인사하다 greeting 명 인사

- The waitress **greeted** us with a big smile. 종업원이 함박웃음을 지으며 우리에게 인사했다.
- Kylie always _____s her teachers politely. Kylie는 항상 선생님들께 공손히 인사한다.

203	**muscle** [mʌ́sl]	명 근육

- Weightlifting can make your **muscles** stronger. 역기를 들면 근육이 더 강해질 수 있다.
- Cycling is good for your leg _____s. 자전거를 타는 것은 다리 근육에 좋다.

204	**reach** [riːtʃ]	동 ~에 이르다/도달하다, (손이) 닿다

- Michelle's hair **reaches** her waist. Michelle의 머리카락은 허리까지 온다.
- Can you _____ the cup on the shelf? 너는 선반 위에 있는 컵을 집을 수 있니?

205	**stairs** [stɛərs]	명 계단

- I fell down on the **stairs** and broke my leg. 나는 계단에서 넘어져서 다리가 부러졌다.
- The _____ in the building are very steep. 그 건물의 계단은 매우 가파르다.

206 abroad

[əbrɔ́:d]

(부) 해외에서, 해외로

• I am not always happy to live **abroad**. 나는 해외에서 사는 것이 항상 행복한 것은 아니다.
• My aunt travels _____ every summer. 우리 고모는 여름마다 해외로 여행을 가신다.

---

207 chin

[tʃin]

(명) 턱

• The boxer was hit on the **chin** and fell down. 그 권투 선수는 턱을 맞고 쓰러졌다.
• The man wiped his daughter's _____ with a napkin.
그 남자는 냅킨으로 딸의 턱을 닦아 주었다.

---

208 local

[lóukəl]

(형) 그 지역의, 근처의

• There are two **local** newspapers in our city. 우리 시에는 두 개의 지역 신문이 있다.
• I enjoy shopping at a _____ market. 나는 근처 시장에서 장보는 것을 좋아한다.

---

209 repair

[ripέər]

(동) 수리하다, 고치다

• The workers are **repairing** the road. 근로자들이 도로를 보수하고 있다.
• My cellphone isn't working. I need to _____ it.
내 휴대전화가 작동하지 않아. 고쳐야 해.

---

210 purse

[pə:rs]

(명) 지갑, 작은 여성용 가방

• Allison took some money out of her **purse**. Allison은 지갑에서 돈을 꺼냈다.
• I left my _____ on the bus. 나는 지갑을 버스에 두고 내렸다.

Check Up

정답 p.118

A 다음 영어단어를 듣고 해당 번호를 쓰시오. 그 다음, 빈칸에 우리말을 쓰시오. 🎧35

challenge ☐   purse ☐   vacation ☐   abroad ☐

_____   _____   _____   _____

flood ☐   muscle ☐   stairs ☐   reach ☐

_____   _____   _____   _____

B 다음 우리말에 해당하는 영어단어를 쓰시오.

1 그 지역의 _____   2 턱 _____

3 수리하다 _____   4 은 _____

5 털 _____   6 인사하다 _____

7 땀을 흘리다 _____

정답 p.118

A 다음 영어단어의 우리말을 쓰시오.

1 monster	_____	2 chest	_____
3 stairs	_____	4 yell	_____
5 silver	_____	6 piece	_____
7 chin	_____	8 vacation	_____
9 invent	_____	10 challenge	_____
11 final	_____	12 flood	_____

B 우리말과 일치하도록 알맞은 영어단어를 써넣어 문장을 완성하시오.

1 Cycling is good for your leg _____s. 자전거를 타는 것은 다리 근육에 좋다.

2 The waitress _____ed us with a big smile. 종업원이 함박웃음을 지으며 우리에게 인사했다.

3 Let's _____ our victory! 우리의 승리를 축하합시다!

4 There are two _____ newspapers in our city. 우리 시에는 두 개의 지역 신문이 있다.

5 These coats are made from animal _____. 이 코트들은 동물의 털로 만들어졌다.

6 The woman kissed her baby on the _____. 그 여자는 아기의 볼에 뽀뽀했다.

7 Allison took some money out of her _____. Allison은 지갑에서 돈을 꺼냈다.

8 Michelle's hair _____es her waist. Michelle의 머리카락은 허리까지 온다.

9 I take a _____ every morning. 나는 매일 아침에 샤워를 한다.

10 It's _____ a beautiful day, isn't it? 너무나 화창한 날이야, 그렇지 않니?

C 다음 영어문장이 우리말과 일치하면 O, 그렇지 않으면 X를 쓰시오.

1 Some people sweat more than others. 어떤 사람들은 다른 사람들보다 땀을 더 많이 흘린다. (   )

2 I am not always happy to live abroad. 나는 해외에서 사는 것이 항상 행복한 것은 아니다. (   )

3 Natalie repaired her hand and asked a question. Natalie는 손을 들고 질문을 했다. (   )

4 Only five minutes survey in the exam. 시험 시간이 5분 밖에 남지 않았다. (   )

5 My dad spread the carpet on the floor. 아빠는 바닥에 카펫을 까셨다. (   )

D 다음 문장을 듣고 문장을 완성한 후, 빈칸에 쓴 영어단어의 우리말을 쓰시오. 🎧36

1 The baseball bat broke into two _____s. ➔ ....

2 We are looking forward to summer _____. ➔ ....

3 Kylie always _____s her teachers politely. ➔ ....

4 Why do you believe _____ things? ➔ ....

5 Please _____ seated during the performance. ➔ ....

6 In most cases, _____ is cheaper than gold. ➔ ....

7 The cat is covered in black _____. ➔ ....

8 Knitting a muffler is a _____ for me. ➔ ....

9 The store _____s its customers every month. ➔ ....

10 What was the _____ score of today's game? ➔ ....

11 Weightlifting can make your _____s stronger. ➔ ....

12 The river was _____ed by the heavy rain. ➔ ....

13 My uniform was wet with _____. ➔ ....

14 There were some old letters in the _____. ➔ ....

15 My tears were running down my _____s. ➔ ....

16 The boxer was hit on the _____ and fell down. ➔ ....

17 The workers are _____ing the road. ➔ ....

18 I was caught in a _____ on my way home. ➔ ....

19 Can you _____ the cup on the shelf? ➔ ....

20 I enjoy shopping at a _____ market. ➔ ....

21 The light bulb was _____ed by Thomas Edition. ➔ ....

22 Americans _____ their independence on July 4. ➔ ....

23 My aunt travels _____ every summer. ➔ ....

24 Mr. Hill _____s cattle on his farm ➔ ....

25 I left my _____ on the bus. ➔ ....

26 The flu can _____ from person to person. ➔ ....

27 I fell down on the _____ and broke my leg. ➔ ....

28 The story is about a big scary _____. ➔ ....

29 "Stop it!" My sister _____ed at me. ➔ ....

30 The girl has a pure _____. ➔ ....

211	**pine** [pain]	몡 소나무, 솔

- The **pine** tree is taller than the oak tree. 그 소나무는 떡갈나무보다 키가 크다.
- Many squirrels live in the _____ forest. 많은 다람쥐들이 소나무 숲에 살고 있다.

212	**screen** [skriːn]	몡 (텔레비전·컴퓨터·영화관의) 화면

- Don't look at the computer **screen** in the dark. 어두운 데서 컴퓨터 화면을 보지 마세요.
- People looked at the _____ when the movie started.
  영화가 시작되자 사람들은 화면을 쳐다보았다.

213	**wing** [wiŋ]	몡 날개

- A bird can fly with its **wings**. 새는 날개로 날 수 있다.
- The ostrich has _____ s, but it cannot fly. 타조는 날개가 있지만 날지 못한다.

214	**seed** [siːd]	몡 씨, 씨앗

- Most fruits have **seeds** inside them. 대부분의 과일에는 씨앗이 들어 있다.
- Most farmers plant _____ s in spring. 대부분의 농부들은 봄에 씨앗을 심는다.

215	**since** [sins]	전 ~부터 접 ~한 때로부터, ~ 때문에

- Ms. Suzuki has lived in Seoul **since** 2010. Suzuki 씨는 2010년부터 서울에서 살고 있다.
- I won't go out _____ it's too hot outside. 밖이 너무 더워서 나는 나가지 않을래.

216	**choir** [kwáiər]	몡 합창단, 성가대

- The school **choir** practices once a week. 교내 합창단은 일주일에 한 번 연습을 한다.
- My sister sings in the church _____ . 내 여동생은 교회 합창단에서 노래를 한다.

217	**hall** [hɔːl]	몡 복도, 홀/넓은 방

- The restroom is at the end of the **hall**. 화장실은 복도 끝에 있다.
- The hotel's _____ can hold 300 people. 그 호텔의 홀은 300명을 수용할 수 있다.

218	**narrow** [nǽrou]	형 (폭이) 좁은

- Drive carefully because the road is **narrow**. 도로가 좁으니 조심해서 운전을 하세요.
- The little girl's shoulders are very _____ . 그 어린 여자아이의 어깨는 매우 좁다.

219	**university** [jùːnəvə́ːrsəti]	몡 대학

- There are many famous **universities** in Boston. 보스턴에는 유명한 대학이 많다.
- Liam went to the top-ranked _____ . Liam은 일류 대학에 들어갔다.

220	**statue** [stǽtʃuː]	몡 조각상

- The sculptor made the **statue** from marble. 그 조각가는 그 조각상을 대리석으로 만들었다.
- The museum has various _____ s. 그 박물관에는 다양한 조각상들이 있다.

221 achieve
[ətʃíːv]

동 이루다, 달성하다
- Do everything to **achieve** your goal. 목표를 이루기 위해 모든 것을 해 보세요.
- Study hard, and you will _____ a good grade.
  열심히 공부하세요, 그러면 좋은 성적을 받을 거예요.

222 chop
[tʃɑp]

동 (음식 재료를) 썰다, (나무를) 자르다
- **Chop** up some vegetables for a salad. 채소를 잘게 썰어서 샐러드를 만드세요.
- The man _____ ped down the tree with an ax. 그 남자는 도끼로 나무를 잘랐다.

223 loss
[lɔ(ː)s]

명 손실, 상실   lose 동 (가지고 있던 것을) 잃다
- My grandfather suffered from memory **loss**. 할아버지는 기억상실증에 걸리셨다.
- The artist's death was a great _____ to our country.
  그 예술가의 죽음은 우리나라의 큰 손실이었다.

224 research
[rísəːrtʃ]

명 연구, 조사   동 연구하다, 조사하다
- The doctor spent his life doing medical **research**. 그 의사는 의학 연구에 일생을 바쳤다.
- My homework is to _____ Shakespeare's life and works.
  내 숙제는 셰익스피어의 생애와 작품을 조사하는 것이다.

225 nearby
[níərbái]

형 가까이의, 근처의
- I saw Aubrey at the **nearby** bank. 나는 근처에 있는 은행에서 Aubrey를 봤다.
- The injured people were sent to a _____ hospital.
  부상을 입은 사람들은 근처 병원으로 보내졌다.

Check Up

정답 p.118

A 다음 영어단어를 듣고 해당 번호를 쓰시오. 그 다음, 빈칸에 우리말을 쓰시오. 🎧38

screen ☐	since ☐	research ☐	achieve ☐
_____	_____	_____	_____
university ☐	nearby ☐	choir ☐	hall ☐
_____	_____	_____	_____

B 다음 우리말에 해당하는 영어단어를 쓰시오.

1 조각상 _____   2 소나무 _____

3 날개 _____   4 씨앗 _____

5 (폭이) 좁은 _____   6 손실, 상실 _____

7 (음식 재료를) 썰다 _____

226	**guest** [gest]	몡 손님, 게스트

• We will have 30 **guests** at the party. 파티에 30명의 손님이 올 것이다.
• Who is the ⬜⬜⬜ on the TV show? 저 TV 쇼의 게스트는 누구니?

227	**cure** [kjuər]	동 치료하다, 치유하다 몡 치료

• The medicine will **cure** your illness. 그 약이 네 병을 치료해 줄 거야.
• There is no ⬜⬜⬜ for a cold. 감기 치료법은 없다.

228	**terrible** [térəbl]	형 끔찍한

• I heard some **terrible** news yesterday. 나는 어제 끔찍한 소식을 들었다.
• The man committed a ⬜⬜⬜ crime. 그 남자는 끔찍한 범죄를 저질렀다.

229	**dive** [daiv]	동 물속으로 (팔과 머리부터) 뛰어들다, 잠수하다

• Don't **dive** into the pool. 수영장으로 뛰어들지 마세요.
• Some whales ⬜⬜⬜ deep in the sea. 어떤 고래들은 바다 깊이 잠수한다.

230	**slim** [slim]	형 날씬한, 얇은

• Nick is **slim**, but his brother is fat. Nick은 날씬하지만, 그의 남동생은 뚱뚱하다.
• This book is ⬜⬜⬜, but it has a lot of information. 이 책은 얇지만 정보가 많다.

231	**clap** [klæp]	동 박수를 치다

• Everyone sang and **clapped** to the music. 모두 음악에 맞춰 노래를 부르며 박수를 쳤다.
• The audience ⬜⬜⬜ped when the show was over. 쇼가 끝나자 관객들이 박수를 쳤다.

232	**heel** [hi:l]	몡 발뒤꿈치, (신발의) 굽

• The shoes are worn down at the **heels**. 그 신발은 뒤꿈치 쪽이 닳았다.
• Erin loves black boots with high ⬜⬜⬜s. Erin은 굽이 높은 검정색 부츠를 좋아한다.

233	**neat** [ni:t]	형 단정한, 정돈된

• Make sure that your clothes look clean and **neat**. 옷이 깨끗하고 단정하게 보이도록 하세요.
• Always keep your room ⬜⬜⬜. 항상 방을 정리된 상태로 유지하세요.

234	**receive** [risíːv]	동 받다

• I **received** an email from George this morning. 오늘 아침에 George에게서 이메일을 받았다.
• I ordered a blue T-shirt but ⬜⬜⬜d a black one.
  나는 파란색 티셔츠를 주문했는데 검은색 티셔츠를 받았다.

235	**straight** [streit]	부 똑바로, 곧장 형 똑바른, 곧은

• Go **straight** and you will find the building. 직진하면 그 건물을 찾을 수 있을 거야.
• Draw a ⬜⬜⬜ line with a ruler. 자를 이용해서 직선을 그리세요.

236 **advertise**
[ǽdvərtàiz]

동 광고하다, 광고를 내다

advertisement 명 광고

- The company **advertised** its new product on TV. 그 회사는 TV를 통해 신제품을 광고했다.
- I _____ d my house for sale online. 나는 집을 팔려고 온라인으로 광고를 냈다.

237 **comfortable**
[kʌ́mfərtəbl]

형 편안한, 안락한

comfort 명 편안함

- Some students feel **comfortable** studying at home.
  어떤 학생들은 집에서 공부하는 것을 편하게 느낀다.
- This sofa is more _____ than that one. 이 소파가 저 소파보다 더 편안하다.

238 **disappear**
[dìsəpíər]

동 (눈에서) 보이지 않게 되다, 사라지다

- The man **disappeared** in the crowd. 그 남자는 사람들 무리 속으로 사라졌다.
- Do you know why dinosaurs _____ ed quickly?
  너는 왜 공룡이 금방 사라졌는지 아니?

239 **medium**
[mí:diəm]

형 중간의

- I like my steak cooked **medium**. 나는 중간 정도로 구운 스테이크를 좋아한다.
- Please give me this shirt in a _____ size. 이 셔츠를 중간 사이즈로 주세요.

240 **respect**
[rispékt]

명 존경, 존중 동 존경하다, 존중하다

- I have **respect** for my grandfather. 나는 우리 할아버지를 존경한다.
- All of them _____ ed their leader's decision. 그들 모두가 지도자의 결정을 존중했다.

Check Up

정답 p.118

A 다음 영어단어를 듣고 해당 번호를 쓰시오. 그 다음, 빈칸에 우리말을 쓰시오. 🎧40

advertise ☐	straight ☐	disappear ☐	comfortable ☐
___	___	___	___
terrible ☐	medium ☐	dive ☐	receive ☐
___	___	___	___

B 다음 우리말에 해당하는 영어단어를 쓰시오.

1 날씬한 _____ 2 손님 _____

3 단정한 _____ 4 박수를 치다 _____

5 존경 _____ 6 발뒤꿈치 _____

7 치료하다 _____

A 다음 영어단어의 우리말을 쓰시오.

1 wing _____   2 dive _____

3 clap _____   4 chop _____

5 terrible _____   6 receive _____

7 narrow _____   8 loss _____

9 pine _____   10 statue _____

11 nearby _____   12 medium _____

B 우리말과 일치하도록 알맞은 영어단어를 써넣어 문장을 완성하시오.

1 Don't look at the computer _____ in the dark. 어두운 데서 컴퓨터 화면을 보지 마세요.

2 Always keep your room _____. 항상 방을 정리된 상태로 유지하세요.

3 Nick is _____, but his brother is fat. Nick은 날씬하지만, 그의 남동생은 뚱뚱하다.

4 This sofa is more _____ than that one. 이 소파가 저 소파보다 더 편안하다.

5 Do everything to _____ your goal. 목표를 이루기 위해 모든 것을 해 보세요.

6 Most fruits have _____s inside them. 대부분의 과일에는 씨앗이 들어 있다.

7 The shoes are worn down at the _____s. 그 신발은 뒤꿈치 쪽이 닳았다.

8 I _____d my house for sale online. 나는 집을 팔려고 온라인으로 광고를 냈다.

9 I have _____ for my grandfather. 나는 우리 할아버지를 존경한다.

10 Ms. Suzuki has lived in Seoul _____ 2010. Suzuki 씨는 2010년부터 서울에서 살고 있다.

C 다음 영어문장이 우리말과 일치하면 O, 그렇지 않으면 X를 쓰시오.

1 Go straight and you will find the building. 직진하면 그 건물을 찾을 수 있을 거야. (   )

2 The man researched in the crowd. 그 남자는 사람들 무리 속으로 사라졌다. (   )

3 We will have 30 halls at the party. 파티에 30명의 손님이 올 것이다. (   )

4 There are many famous universities in Boston. 보스턴에는 유명한 대학이 많다. (   )

5 The medicine will cure your illness. 그 약이 네 병을 치료해 줄 거야. (   )

D 다음 문장을 듣고 문장을 완성한 후, 빈칸에 쓴 영어단어의 우리말을 쓰시오. 🎧41

1 A bird can fly with its _____s. ➡ ....

2 I saw Aubrey at the _____ bank. ➡ ....

3 Most farmers plant _____s in spring. ➡ ....

4 This book is _____, but it has a lot of information. ➡ ....

5 There is no _____ for a cold. ➡ ....

6 Who is the _____ on the TV show? ➡ ....

7 All of them _____ed their leader's decision. ➡ ....

8 I won't go out _____ it's too hot outside. ➡ ....

9 Everyone sang and _____ped to the music. ➡ ....

10 I heard some _____ news yesterday. ➡ ....

11 My sister sings in the church _____. ➡ ....

12 Draw a _____ line with a ruler. ➡ ....

13 Don't _____ into the pool. ➡ ....

14 Liam went to the top-ranked _____. ➡ ....

15 The company _____d its new product on TV. ➡ ....

16 People looked at the _____ when the movie started. ➡ ....

17 My grandfather suffered from memory _____. ➡ ....

18 Drive carefully because the road is _____. ➡ ....

19 I like my steak cooked _____. ➡ ....

20 Some students feel _____ studying at home. ➡ ....

21 The sculptor made the _____ from marble. ➡ ....

22 Erin loves black boots with high _____s. ➡ ....

23 Do you know why dinosaurs _____ed quickly? ➡ ....

24 The restroom is at the end of the _____. ➡ ....

25 My homework is to _____ Shakespeare's life and works. ➡ ....

26 Study hard, and you will _____ a good grade. ➡ ....

27 Make sure that your clothes look clean and _____. ➡ ....

28 The man _____ped down the tree with an ax. ➡ ....

29 I _____d an email from George this morning. ➡ ....

30 The _____ tree is taller than the oak tree. ➡ ....

241 height
[hait]

(명) 높이, 키

high (형) 높은

- The **height** of the building is over 100 meters. 그 건물의 높이는 100미터가 넘는다.
- My sister is almost the same ⬚⬚⬚⬚⬚⬚ as me. 내 여동생은 나와 거의 키가 같다.

---

242 pop
[pɑp]

(동) (펑 하는 소리를 내며) 터지다, 터트리다

- We are waiting for the popcorn to **pop**. 우리는 팝콘이 터지기를 기다리고 있다.
- A boy ⬚⬚⬚⬚⬚ped the balloon with a pin. 한 남자아이가 핀으로 풍선을 터트렸다.

---

243 through
[θruː]

(전) ~을 통해, 관통하여

- A scientist is looking **through** a microscope. 과학자가 현미경을 들여다보고 있다.
- A woman is walking ⬚⬚⬚⬚⬚⬚ the woods. 한 여자가 숲을 통과하여 걷고 있다.

---

244 dot
[dɑt]

(명) (동그란 작은) 점

- The socks are black with white **dots**. 그 양말은 검정색에 흰 점들이 있다.
- Connect all the ⬚⬚⬚⬚⬚s to find the picture.
  그림을 알아볼 수 있도록 모든 점을 연결하시오.

---

245 soil
[sɔil]

(명) 흙, 토양

- Plants need **soil**, water, and sunlight to live. 식물은 살기 위해 흙, 물, 그리고 햇빛이 필요하다.
- Put some more ⬚⬚⬚⬚⬚ in the flower pot. 화분에 흙을 좀 더 넣으세요.

---

246 complain
[kəmpléin]

(동) 불평하다, 항의하다

- Mr. Lopez never **complains** about his job. Lopez 씨는 자신의 일에 대해 절대 불평하지 않는다.
- Some customers ⬚⬚⬚⬚⬚ed about their food. 일부 고객들이 음식에 대해 항의했다.

---

247 hesitate
[hézitèit]

(동) 망설이다, 머뭇거리다

- If you have any questions, don't **hesitate** to ask. 질문이 있으면 망설이지 말고 물어보세요.
- Emma ⬚⬚⬚⬚⬚d to talk to others. Emma는 다른 사람과 이야기하는 것을 주저했다.

---

248 necessary
[nésəsèri]

(형) 필요한

necessarily (부) 필히

- A passport is **necessary** to travel abroad. 해외로 여행을 가려면 여권이 필요하다.
- Water is ⬚⬚⬚⬚⬚ for life. 물은 모든 생물에 필요하다.

---

249 recommend
[rèkəménd]

(동) 추천하다

recommendation (명) 추천

- Can you **recommend** a Thai restaurant? 너는 태국 음식을 파는 식당을 추천해 줄 수 있니?
- A friend of mine ⬚⬚⬚⬚⬚ed this movie to me. 내 친구 한 명이 이 영화를 추천했다.

---

250 strike
[straik]
strike-struck-stricken

(동) (강하게) 치다, 부딪치다

- Lightning **struck** a tall pine tree last night. 어젯밤에 번개가 키 큰 소나무를 내리쳤다.
- A car ⬚⬚⬚⬚⬚ the wall. 차가 벽에 부딪쳤다.

251　**aisle**
[ail]

(명) 통로

• Would you like a window seat or an **aisle** seat?
창가 쪽 좌석을 원하시나요, 아니면 통로 쪽 좌석을 원하시나요?

• You can find the eggs at the end of the _____ . 계란은 통로 끝에서 찾으실 수 있습니다.

252　**community**
[kəmjúːnəti]

(명) 지역 공동체, (같은 관심사 등의) 모임

• The doctor is very famous in this **community**. 그 의사는 지역 사회에서 매우 유명하다.

• A young scientist surprised the scientific _____ .
한 젊은 과학자가 과학계를 놀라게 했다.

253　**disappoint**
[dìsəpɔ́int]

(동) 실망시키다

• Don't **disappoint** me once again. 나를 또 다시 실망시키지는 마.

• I'm _____ ed with your behavior. 나는 너의 행동에 실망했어.

254　**metal**
[métəl]

(명) 금속

• Every type of **metal** sinks in the water. 모든 금속은 물에 가라앉는다.

• Iron is one of the most widely used _____ s. 철은 가장 널리 사용되는 금속 중 하나이다.

255　**row**
[róu]

(명) 줄, 열

• About 30 people are lined up in a **row**. 약 30명의 사람들이 한 줄로 서 있다.

• I hate to sit in the front _____ at the movies.
나는 극장에서 맨 앞줄에 앉는 것을 싫어한다.

Check Up

정답 p.119

A 다음 영어단어를 듣고 해당 번호를 쓰시오. 그 다음, 빈칸에 우리말을 쓰시오. 🎧43

disappoint ☐　recommend ☐　hesitate ☐　height ☐

_____　_____　_____　_____

through ☐　community ☐　pop ☐　necessary ☐

_____　_____　_____　_____

B 다음 우리말에 해당하는 영어단어를 쓰시오.

1 통로　_____　　2 금속　_____

3 줄, 열　_____　　4 (강하게) 치다　_____

5 (동그란 작은) 점　_____　　6 흙　_____

7 불평하다　_____

256 excuse
[ikskjúːs]

⑧ 용서하다　⑨ 이유, 변명
- Please **excuse** me for being rude. 제가 무례했던 점은 용서해 주세요.
- What's your _____ for being late? 너는 늦은 이유가 뭐니?

257 poster
[póustər]

⑨ 벽보, 포스터
- A man is putting up **posters** on the wall. 한 남자가 벽에 벽보를 붙이고 있다.
- The _____ advertises a magic show. 그 포스터는 마술쇼를 광고하고 있다.

258 tie
[tai]

⑧ (끈 등으로) 매다, 묶다　⑨ 넥타이
- Jane **tied** her dog to a tree for a moment. Jane은 잠시 개를 나무에 묶어 두었다.
- The blue _____ matches the suit well. 파란 넥타이는 그 정장과 잘 어울린다.

259 enemy
[énəmi]

⑨ 적
- France and Germany were **enemies** for a long time. 프랑스와 독일은 오랫동안 적이었다.
- I'm your friend, not your _____. 난 너의 적이 아니라 친구야.

260 soldier
[sóuldʒər]

⑨ 군인
- Millions of **soldiers** died in the First World War.
  제1차 세계 대전에서 수백만 명의 군인들이 목숨을 잃었다.
- _____s must be ready to fight at all times. 군인들은 항상 싸울 준비가 되어 있어야 한다.

261 complete
[kəmplíːt]

⑧ 완성하다, 끝내다　⑨ 완전한, 부족함이 없는
- It took two hours to **complete** the work. 그 일을 끝내는 데 2시간이 걸렸다.
- This is not a _____ sentence. 이것은 완전한 문장이 아니다.

262 household
[háushòuld]

⑨ 가정
- Almost every **household** has a computer. 거의 모든 가정에 컴퓨터가 있다.
- I always try to help with _____ work. 나는 항상 집안일을 도우려고 한다.

263 nervous
[nə́ːrvəs]

⑨ 긴장한, 두려워하는
- I get **nervous** when I speak in public. 나는 사람들 앞에서 말할 때 긴장을 한다.
- The final exam made all of us very _____. 기말 시험은 우리 모두를 긴장하게 했다.

264 reduce
[ridjúːs]

⑧ (수·양 등을) 줄이다, 감소시키다
- We need to **reduce** food waste. 우리는 음식물 쓰레기의 양을 줄여야 한다.
- The company _____d the price of the product. 그 회사는 제품의 가격을 낮추었다.

265 structure
[strʌ́ktʃər]

⑨ 구조, 구조물/건축물
- The brain has a very complex **structure**. 뇌는 매우 복잡한 구조를 가지고 있다.
- We will build a huge steel _____. 우리는 거대한 철골 건축물을 만들 것이다.

266 allow
[əláu]

(동) 허락하다, 허가하다

- The security guard didn't **allow** us to enter the building.
  경비원이 우리를 건물에 들어가지 못하게 했다.
- Taking pictures is not _____ed in the museum.
  박물관에서의 사진 촬영은 허가되지 않는다.

---

267 compare
[kəmpέər]

(동) 비교하다

- I **compared** two skirts and bought one. 나는 두 벌의 치마를 비교해 보고 하나를 구입했다.
- Don't _____ yourself with others. 네 자신을 다른 사람과 비교하지 마라.

---

268 discount
[dískaunt]

(명) 할인   (동) 할인하다

- Book early and get a **discount**. 일찍 예약을 하고 할인을 받으세요.
- All items here are _____ed by 30%. 여기에 있는 모든 제품들은 30%까지 할인됩니다.

---

269 modern
[mádərn]

(형) 현대의, 현대적인

- The Internet has a huge effect on **modern** society. 인터넷은 현대 사회에 큰 영향을 미친다.
- The new building looks _____ and beautiful. 그 새 건물은 현대적이고 아름다워 보인다.

---

270 rumor
[rú:mər]

(명) 소문, 루머

- According to the **rumor**, the factory will be closed soon.
  소문에 의하면, 그 공장은 곧 문을 닫을 것이다.
- There is a _____ that the man is a millionaire. 그 남자가 백만장자라는 소문이 있다.

Check Up

정답 p.119

Ⓐ 다음 영어단어를 듣고 해당 번호를 쓰시오. 그 다음, 빈칸에 우리말을 쓰시오. 🎧45

discount ☐	structure ☐	reduce ☐	nervous ☐
_____	_____	_____	_____
complete ☐	compare ☐	household ☐	modern ☐
_____	_____	_____	_____

Ⓑ 다음 우리말에 해당하는 영어단어를 쓰시오.

1 적 _____
2 허락하다 _____

3 소문 _____
4 군인 _____

5 벽보 _____
6 (끈 등으로) 매다 _____

7 변명 _____

A 다음 영어단어의 우리말을 쓰시오.

1 dot _____   2 enemy _____

3 soldier _____   4 rumor _____

5 modern _____   6 household _____

7 complain _____   8 height _____

9 compare _____   10 nervous _____

11 aisle _____   12 hesitate _____

B 우리말과 일치하도록 알맞은 영어단어를 써넣어 문장을 완성하시오.

1 We need to _____ food waste. 우리는 음식물 쓰레기의 양을 줄여야 한다.

2 The brain has a very complex _____. 뇌는 매우 복잡한 구조를 가지고 있다.

3 Every type of _____ sinks in the water. 모든 금속은 물에 가라앉는다.

4 What's your _____ for being late? 너는 늦은 이유가 뭐니?

5 I'm _____ed with your behavior. 나는 너의 행동에 실망했어.

6 Book early and get a _____. 일찍 예약을 하고 할인을 받으세요.

7 Jane _____d her dog to a tree for a moment. Jane은 잠시 개를 나무에 묶어 두었다.

8 Lightning _____ a tall pine tree last night. 어젯밤에 번개가 키 큰 소나무를 내리쳤다.

9 About 30 people are lined up in a _____. 약 30명의 사람들이 한 줄로 서 있다.

10 Put some more _____ in the flower pot. 화분에 흙을 좀 더 넣으세요.

C 다음 영어문장이 우리말과 일치하면 O, 그렇지 않으면 X를 쓰시오.

1 A boy recommended the balloon with a pin. 한 남자아이가 핀으로 풍선을 터뜨렸다. (   )

2 Taking pictures is not allowed in the museum. 박물관에서의 사진 촬영은 허가되지 않는다. (   )

3 This is not a complete sentence. 이것은 완전한 문장이 아니다. (   )

4 A scientist is looking through a microscope. 과학자가 현미경을 들여다보고 있다. (   )

5 Water is modern for life. 물은 모든 생명에 필요하다. (   )

D 다음 문장을 듣고 문장을 완성한 후, 빈칸에 쓴 영어단어의 우리말을 쓰시오. 🎧46

1 Plants need _____, water, and sunlight to live. → ....

2 Can you _____ a Thai restaurant? → ....

3 The _____ of the building is over 100 meters. → ....

4 The doctor is very famous in this _____. → ....

5 A car _____ the wall. → ....

6 All items here are _____ed by 30%. → ....

7 We are waiting for the popcorn to _____. → ....

8 Don't _____ me once again. → ....

9 A man is putting up _____s on the wall. → ....

10 The socks are black with white _____s. → ....

11 The Internet has a huge effect on _____ society. → ....

12 Would you like a window seat or an _____ seat? → ....

13 A woman is walking _____ the woods. → ....

14 Mr. Lopez never _____s about his job. → ....

15 I always try to help with _____ work. → ....

16 Taking pictures is not _____ed in the museum. → ....

17 There is a _____ that the man is a millionaire. → ....

18 If you have any questions, don't _____ to ask. → ....

19 The blue _____ matches the suit well. → ....

20 Iron is one of the most widely used _____s. → ....

21 Please _____ me for being rude. → ....

22 I get _____ when I speak in public. → ....

23 I hate to sit in the front _____ at the movies. → ....

24 A passport is _____ to travel abroad. → ....

25 It took two hours to _____ the work. → ....

26 We will build a huge steel _____. → ....

27 I'm your friend, not your _____. → ....

28 Don't _____ yourself with others. → ....

29 The company _____d the price of the product. → ....

30 Millions of _____s died in the First World War. → ....

| 271 | **ill**
[il] | 阌 아픈, 병에 걸린 | illness 阌 병 |

- I felt **ill** yesterday but fine today. 나는 어제 아팠지만 오늘은 괜찮다.
- Kevin has been ▨▨▨▨ in bed since last week. Kevin은 지난주부터 앓아누워 있다.

| 272 | **speech**
[spiːtʃ] | 阌 연설, 강연 | speak 阌 말하다 |

- His **speech** was very boring. 그의 연설은 매우 지루했다.
- The principal gave us a ▨▨▨▨. 교장선생님이 우리에게 연설하셨다.

| 273 | **tired**
[taiərd] | 阌 지친, 피곤한 | tire 阌 지치게 하다, 피곤하게 하다 |

- After a long journey, the man looked **tired**. 오랜 여행 후에 그 남자는 지쳐 보였다.
- I was very ▨▨▨▨, so I went to bed early. 나는 매우 피곤해서 일찍 잠자리에 들었다.

| 274 | **equal**
[íːkwəl] | 阌 (수·양·가치 등이) 같은, 동등한/평등한 |

- I cut the apple pie into six **equal** pieces. 나는 사과 파이를 같은 크기의 6조각으로 잘랐다.
- Everyone has an ▨▨▨▨ right to vote. 모든 사람들은 동등한 투표권을 가지고 있다.

| 275 | **square**
[skwɛər] | 阌 정사각형   阌 정사각형의 |

- A **square** has four angles. 정사각형은 네 개의 각이 있다.
- We bought a ▨▨▨▨ table. 우리는 정사각형 테이블을 샀다.

| 276 | **confident**
[kánfidənt] | 阌 자신감 있는, 확신하는 | confidence 阌 확신 |

- Heather is **confident** about her writing skills. Heather는 글쓰기에 자신감이 있다.
- I'm ▨▨▨▨ of your success. 나는 너의 성공을 확신해.

| 277 | **hug**
[hʌg] | 阌 끌어안다, 포옹하다   阌 포옹 |

- I **hugged** my mom when she came home. 엄마가 집에 오셨을 때 나는 엄마를 껴안았다.
- Henry gave his daughter a ▨▨▨▨. Henry는 딸을 끌어안았다.

| 278 | **nod**
[nɑd] | 阌 (고개를) 끄덕이다 |

- The teacher **nodded** when I gave the right answer.
내가 정답을 말하자 선생님은 고개를 끄덕이셨다.
- Jane ▨▨▨▨ded her head to greet me. Jane은 나에게 인사하려고 고개를 끄덕였다.

| 279 | **relieve**
[rilíːv] | 阌 (고통 등을) 줄이다, 완화시키다 |

- This pill will **relieve** your pain. 이 약이 당신의 통증을 줄여줄 것입니다.
- A massage can help ▨▨▨▨ tension. 마사지는 긴장을 푸는 데 도움이 된다.

| 280 | **sunshine**
[sʌ́nʃàin] | 阌 햇빛 |

- In spring, we can enjoy a lot of **sunshine**. 봄에는 많은 양의 햇빛을 즐길 수 있다.
- Too much ▨▨▨▨ may cause sunburn. 과도한 햇빛은 화상의 원인이 될 수 있다.

281 amazing
[əméiziŋ]

(형) 놀라운, 굉장한

amaze (동) 놀라게 하다

- The explorer had an **amazing** experience in the jungle.
  그 탐험가는 정글에서 놀라운 경험을 했다.
- The man is an ⬜⬜⬜⬜⬜ dancer. 그 남자는 굉장한 춤꾼이다.

282 confuse
[kənfjúːz]

(동) 헷갈리게 하다, 혼동하다

confusion (명) 혼란

- Words like *lay* and *lie* always **confuse** me. 'lay'와 'lie'와 같은 단어들은 항상 헷갈린다.
- Never ⬜⬜⬜⬜⬜ facts and opinions. 사실과 의견을 절대 혼동하지 마세요.

283 edge
[edʒ]

(명) 가장자리/모서리, (칼 등의) 날

- The boy is sitting on the **edge** of the sofa. 그 남자아이는 소파의 모서리에 앉아 있다.
- The knife has a sharp ⬜⬜⬜⬜⬜ and cuts well. 그 칼은 날이 날카로워서 잘 든다.

284 native
[néitiv]

(형) 태어난 곳의 (명) ~ 태생/출신인 사람

- The immigrant misses his **native** country. 그 이민자는 모국을 그리워한다.
- Mr. McLean is a ⬜⬜⬜⬜⬜ of Australia. McLean 씨는 호주 태생이다.

285 separate
[sépərit]

(형) 따로 떨어진 (동) 분리하다 [sépəreit]

separately (부) 각각

- The family members live in **separate** countries. 그 가족들은 각기 다른 나라에서 살고 있다.
- ⬜⬜⬜⬜⬜ the egg yolk from the white. 달걀노른자와 흰자를 분리하세요.

Check Up

정답 p.120

A 다음 영어단어를 듣고 해당 번호를 쓰시오. 그 다음, 빈칸에 우리말을 쓰시오. 🎧48

sunshine ⬜	separate ⬜	confuse ⬜	relieve ⬜
___	___	___	___
confident ⬜	ill ⬜	native ⬜	speech ⬜
___	___	___	

B 다음 우리말에 해당하는 영어단어를 쓰시오.

1 (수·양·가치 등이) 같은 _____   2 가장자리 _____

3 놀라운 _____   4 (고개를) 끄덕이다 _____

5 정사각형 _____   6 끌어안다 _____

7 지친 _____

49

286	**instead** [instéd]	彫 대신에

- I don't like chicken. I'll have pizza **instead**. 나는 치킨을 좋아하지 않아. 대신에 피자를 먹을게.
- The white caps were sold out, so I bought a grey one _____.
  흰색 모자가 다 팔려서 나는 그 대신에 회색 모자를 샀다.

287	**protect** [prətékt]	動 보호하다	protection 名 보호

- We should **protect** our eyes from the sun. 우리는 태양으로부터 눈을 보호해야 한다.
- We must _____ our Earth. 우리는 지구를 보호해야 한다.

288	**title** [táitl]	名 제목

- What is the **title** of the book? 그 책의 제목이 뭐니?
- I can't remember the _____ of the movie. 나는 그 영화의 제목이 생각나질 않는다.

289	**flight** [flait]	名 비행, 비행기(편)	fly 動 날다, 비행하다

- Ms. Brown took pictures of birds in **flight**. Brown 씨는 하늘을 나는 새들의 사진을 찍었다.
- The _____ for Rome will leave at 11 a.m. 로마행 비행기는 오전 11시에 출발할 것이다.

290	**stamp** [stæmp]	名 우표, 도장

- Don't forget to put a **stamp** on the letter. 편지에 우표 붙이는 것을 잊지 마세요.
- Lily has many _____s in her passport. Lily의 여권에는 많은 도장이 찍혀 있다.

291	**contact** [kántækt]	名 (신체적인) 접촉, 연락　動 접촉하다, 연락하다

- The disease is caused by **contact** with animals. 그 질병은 동물과의 접촉으로 발생한다.
- Please _____ us if you need more information. 정보가 좀 더 필요하시면 연락하세요.

292	**improve** [imprú:v]	動 나아지다, 향상시키다

- His health is **improving** day by day. 그의 건강은 서서히 나아지고 있다.
- How can I _____ my grade in math? 내가 어떻게 하면 수학 점수를 높일 수 있을까?

293	**officer** [ɔ́(ː)fisər]	名 장교, 공무원/관리

- Navy **officers** wear white uniforms and caps. 해군 장교들은 흰색 제복과 모자를 착용한다.
- My uncle is an _____ of the city government. 우리 삼촌은 시청 공무원이시다.

294	**respond** [rispánd]	動 응답하다, 반응하다	response 名 반응

- William didn't **respond** to my email. William은 내 이메일에 답하지 않았다.
- Chameleons _____ quickly to colors. 카멜레온은 색깔에 빠르게 반응한다.

295	**surface** [sə́ːrfis]	名 표면

- The **surface** of the Moon looks very rocky. 달의 표면은 울퉁불퉁해 보인다.
- Water lilies float on the _____ of water. 수련은 수면 위를 떠다닌다.

296 **amount**
[əmáunt]
명 (무엇의) 양
- Most elephants eat a large **amount** of food. 대부분의 코끼리는 엄청난 양의 먹이를 먹는다.
- Eat the right _____ of food at the right time. 적당한 때에 적당한 양의 음식을 드세요.

297 **continent**
[kántinənt]
명 대륙
- There are five oceans and seven **continents** on Earth.
  지구에는 5개의 대양과 7개의 대륙이 있다.
- The smallest _____ is Australia. 가장 작은 대륙은 호주이다.

298 **education**
[èdʒukéiʃən]
명 교육
educate 통 교육시키다
- The artist had almost no formal **education**. 그 화가는 정식 교육을 거의 받지 못했다.
- Many countries offer free _____ to students.
  많은 국가들이 학생들에게 무상 교육을 제공한다.

299 **normal**
[nɔ́ːrməl]
형 보통의, 일반적인
- **Normal** working hours are nine hours a day. 일반적인 근무 시간은 하루에 9시간이다.
- It is _____ to use chopsticks to eat in Korea.
  한국에서는 젓가락을 사용해서 식사를 하는 것이 일반적이다.

300 **sight**
[sait]
명 시력, 광경
see 통 보다
- Anne wears glasses because of poor **sight**. Anne은 시력이 좋지 않아서 안경을 쓴다.
- A rainbow over the sea is a very beautiful _____.
  바다 위로 뜬 무지개는 매우 멋진 광경이다.

Check Up
정답 p.120

A 다음 영어단어를 듣고 해당 번호를 쓰시오. 그 다음, 빈칸에 우리말을 쓰시오. 🎧50

education ☐   officer ☐   surface ☐   respond ☐

_____   _____   _____   _____

amount ☐   improve ☐   contact ☐   continent ☐

_____   _____   _____   _____

B 다음 우리말에 해당하는 영어단어를 쓰시오.

1 우표 _____   2 시력 _____

3 제목 _____   4 대신에 _____

5 보통의 _____   6 보호하다 _____

7 비행 _____

정답 p.120

A 다음 영어단어의 우리말을 쓰시오.

1 respond _____   2 instead _____

3 protect _____   4 surface _____

5 flight _____   6 nod _____

7 continent _____   8 edge _____

9 tired _____   10 amount _____

11 education _____   12 stamp _____

B 우리말과 일치하도록 알맞은 영어단어를 써넣어 문장을 완성하시오.

1 _____ the egg yolk from the white.   달걀노른자와 흰자를 <u>분리하세요</u>.

2 Too much _____ may cause sunburn.   과도한 <u>햇빛</u>은 화상의 원인이 될 수 있다.

3 Everyone has an _____ right to vote.   모든 사람들은 <u>동등한</u> 투표권을 가지고 있다.

4 What is the _____ of the book?   그 책의 <u>제목</u>이 뭐니?

5 Never _____ facts and opinions.   사실과 의견을 절대 <u>혼동하지</u> 마세요.

6 Mr. McLean is a _____ of Australia.   McLean 씨는 호주 <u>태생이다</u>.

7 A _____ has four angles.   <u>정사각형</u>은 네 개의 각이 있다.

8 The disease is caused by _____ with animals.   그 질병은 동물과의 <u>접촉으로</u> 발생한다.

9 _____ working hours are nine hours a day.   <u>일반적인</u> 근무 시간은 하루에 9시간이다.

10 His _____ was very boring.   그의 <u>연설</u>은 매우 지루했다.

C 다음 영어문장이 우리말과 일치하면 O, 그렇지 않으면 X를 쓰시오.

1 Henry gave his daughter a hug.   Henry는 딸을 끌어안았다. (   )

2 His health is improving day by day.   그의 건강은 서서히 나아지고 있다. (   )

3 A massage can help relieve tension.   마사지는 긴장을 푸는 데 도움이 된다. (   )

4 I felt confident yesterday but fine today.   나는 어제 아팠지만 오늘은 괜찮다. (   )

5 The man is an amazing dancer.   그 남자는 굉장한 춤꾼이다. (   )

D 다음 문장을 듣고 문장을 완성한 후, 빈칸에 쓴 영어단어의 우리말을 쓰시오. 🎧51

1 Anne wears glasses because of poor _____. ➡ ....

2 The _____ of the Moon looks very rocky. ➡ ....

3 Don't forget to put a _____ on the letter. ➡ ....

4 The principal gave us a _____. ➡ ....

5 The family members live in _____ countries. ➡ ....

6 After a long journey, the man looked _____. ➡ ....

7 Kevin has been _____ in bed since last week. ➡ ....

8 Ms. Brown took pictures of birds in _____. ➡ ....

9 The immigrant misses his _____ country. ➡ ....

10 It is _____ to use chopsticks to eat in Korea. ➡ ....

11 I don't like chicken. I'll have pizza _____. ➡ ....

12 Please _____ us if you need more information. ➡ ....

13 This pill will _____ your pain. ➡ ....

14 We must _____ our Earth. ➡ ....

15 Eat the right _____ of food at the right time. ➡ ....

16 Heather is _____ about her writing skills. ➡ ....

17 The knife has a sharp _____ and cuts well. ➡ ....

18 Words like *lay* and *lie* always _____ me. ➡ ....

19 The smallest _____ is Australia. ➡ ....

20 The teacher _____ded when I gave the right answer. ➡ ....

21 Navy _____s wear white uniforms and caps. ➡ ....

22 I _____ged my mom when she came home. ➡ ....

23 How can I _____ my grade in math? ➡ ....

24 The explorer had an _____ experience in the jungle. ➡ ....

25 I cut the apple pie into six _____ pieces. ➡ ....

26 William didn't _____ to my email. ➡ ....

27 In spring, we can enjoy a lot of _____. ➡ ....

28 We bought a _____ table. ➡ ....

29 I can't remember the _____ of the movie. ➡ ....

30 The artist had almost no formal _____. ➡ ....

A 영어단어는 우리말로, 우리말은 영어단어로 바꿔 쓰시오.

1 forgive	→	26 제한하다	→
2 manner	→	27 벌을 주다	→
3 repair	→	28 녹다	→
4 announce	→	29 공정한	→
5 possible	→	30 축하하다	→
6 miracle	→	31 사회	→
7 wonder	→	32 준비하다	→
8 surface	→	33 햇빛	→
9 underground	→	34 포함하다	→
10 muscle	→	35 우표	→
11 reply	→	36 연못	→
12 behavior	→	37 빛나다	→
13 yell	→	38 발표하다, 알리다	→
14 stretch	→	39 은	→
15 order	→	40 계단	→
16 abroad	→	41 턱	→
17 amount	→	42 습한	→
18 physical	→	43 인사하다	→
19 university	→	44 무시하다	→
20 achieve	→	45 정사각형	→
21 nearby	→	46 설문 조사	→
22 receive	→	47 박수를 치다	→
23 main	→	48 흙	→
24 complain	→	49 가격	→
25 recommend	→	50 현대의	→

B 우리말과 일치하도록 알맞은 영어단어를 써넣어 문장을 완성하시오.

1 We could _____ the airport on time. 우리는 정시에 공항에 도착할 수 있었다.

2 The man dug a _____ with a shovel. 그 남자는 삽으로 구멍을 팠다.

3 The speaker is pointing at the _____. 연설자가 화면을 가리키고 있다.

4 I was so _____ that I fell asleep on the bus. 나는 매우 피곤해서 버스에서 잠이 들었다.

5 The glass was set on the _____ of the table. 유리잔이 탁자 모서리에 놓여 있었다.

6 The road is too _____ for a car to pass. 그 길은 폭이 너무 좁아서 자동차가 지나갈 수 없다.

7 The disease will be _____d sooner or later. 그 질병은 조만간 치료될 것이다.

8 Dogs have a good _____ of smell. 개들은 후각이 뛰어나다.

9 What will you do during the summer _____? 너는 여름 방학 동안 무엇을 할 거니?

10 My sister went out, but I _____ed at home. 언니는 나갔지만, 나는 집에 남아 있었다.

11 The weather was _____ throughout the week. 한 주 내내 날씨가 매우 나빴다.

12 I'll go _____ home after school. 나는 방과 후에 곧바로 집에 갈 거야.

13 Laura _____d the string around the giftbox. Laura는 선물상자를 끈으로 묶었다.

14 Place the frying pan over _____ heat. 중간 불에 프라이팬을 올려놓으세요.

15 The man won a _____ dollars in the lottery. 그 남자는 복권에 당첨되어 백만 달러를 탔다.

16 _____s are expected on Tuesday. 화요일에 소나기가 올 것으로 예상된다.

17 Please _____ through your nose. 코로 숨을 쉬어 보세요.

18 This exercise will make you _____ a lot. 이 운동은 땀이 많이 나게 할 거야.

19 Fixing the computer by myself was a _____. 혼자서 컴퓨터를 고치는 건 힘든 일이었어.

20 The _____ news airs at 6 p.m. daily. 지역 뉴스는 매일 저녁 6시에 방송한다.

21 I keep in _____ with my elementary school friends. 나는 초등학교 친구들과 연락을 하고 지낸다.

22 I ate three _____s of cheesecake. 나는 세 조각의 치즈 케이크를 먹었다.

23 The news _____ quickly around the world. 그 뉴스는 전 세계로 빠르게 퍼져 나갔다.

24 The general was highly _____ed by the soldiers. 그 장군은 병사들에게 매우 존경받았다.

25 The _____ cannot be true. 그 소문은 사실일 리가 없다.

C 다음 문장에 들어갈 알맞은 단어를 고르시오.

1 The brothers always [argue / shake / volunteer] with each other.

2 Chocolate was [producing / melting / grabbing] in my fingers.

3 The restroom is at the end of the [hole / structure / hall].

4 [Separate / Normal / Tired] working hours are nine hours a day.

5 The teacher [relieved / nodded / compared] when I gave the right answer.

6 We need to [reduce / complete / excuse] food waste.

7 The teacher [relaxed / explained / pretended] some rules to us.

8 About 30 people are lined up in a [soil / heel / row].

9 The sculptor made the [stairs / statue / sheet] from marble.

10 Weightlifting can make your [chin / sweat / muscles] stronger.

11 The town was totally destroyed by the [flood / survey / choir].

12 Natalie [relieved / raised / responded] her hand and asked a question.

13 How can I [protect / improve / allow] my grade in math?

14 Don't [compare / count / complete] yourself with others.

15 I get [nervous / equal / normal] when I speak in public.

16 You must not park your [vehicle / award / spirit] here.

17 There are five oceans and seven [communities / continents / caves] on Earth.

18 I have a [modern / confident / sore] throat with the flu.

19 I was [punished / cured / challenged] for fighting with my brother.

20 Nick is [neat / slim / comfortable], but his brother is fat.

21 The man [disappeared / discounted / disappointed] in the crowd.

22 The baseball game was [weighed / canceled / experienced] because of the weather.

23 Every type of [hole / metal / aisle] sinks in the water.

24 Most vehicles have two or four [wheels / wings / seeds].

25 The population of our country is [recognizing / chasing / increasing].

D 다음 단어의 바뀐 품사를 보기 에서 찾아 빈칸에 쓰고, 그 단어의 우리말을 쓰시오.

보기	breath	intelligence	educate	illness	finally
	confidence	celebration	separately	protection	fly
	advertisement	comfort	high	necessarily	see

1 형 necessary → 부 _____ → ....

2 형 intelligent → 명 _____ → ....

3 형 separate → 부 _____ → ....

4 형 final → 부 _____ → ....

5 동 breathe → 명 _____ → ....

6 동 advertise → 명 _____ → ....

7 형 confident → 명 _____ → ....

8 명 height → 형 _____ → ....

9 명 education → 동 _____ → ....

10 형 ill → 명 _____ → ....

11 명 sight → 동 _____ → ....

12 형 comfortable → 명 _____ → ....

13 동 protect → 명 _____ → ....

14 명 flight → 동 _____ → ....

15 동 celebrate → 명 _____ → ....

❶ TIP

few와 little은 둘 다 '거의 없는'이라는 부정적인 의미를 나타내지만, few는 셀 수 있는 명사와 함께 쓰이고, little은 셀 수 없는 명사와 함께 쓰입니다.

✰ **Few students knew his name.** —— 그의 이름을 아는 학생은 거의 없다.

✰ **There is very little money left.** —— 남은 돈이 정말 거의 없다.

301	**joke** [ʤouk]	몧 농담 통 농담하다

- Everybody laughed at my **joke**. 내 농담에 모든 사람들이 웃었다.
- Mr. Baker made some _____s before his speech.
  Baker 씨는 연설 전에 몇 가지 농담을 했다.

302	**public** [pʌ́blik]	몧 일반인들, 대중 휑 일반인의, 모두를 위한/공공의

- The picture will be open to the **public** soon. 그 그림은 곧 일반인들에게 공개될 것이다.
- We can use the _____ library for free. 우리는 공공도서관을 무료로 이용할 수 있다.

303	**toward** [tɔːrd]	젼 ~쪽으로, ~을 향하여

- Visitors are walking **toward** the lobby. 방문객들이 로비 쪽으로 걸어가고 있다.
- Most plants grow _____ the sunlight. 대부분의 식물들은 햇빛을 향해 자란다.

304	**fold** [fould]	통 (옷·종이 등을) 접다

- **Fold** your T-shirts and put them in the drawer. 네 티셔츠들을 개어 서랍에 넣어라.
- Let's _____ the colored paper into a ball. 색종이를 접어서 공을 만들자.

305	**stream** [striːm]	몧 개울, 시내

- The **stream** flows into a larger river. 그 개울은 더 큰 강으로 흘러간다.
- The _____ is shallow. You can walk across it. 그 개울은 얕아. 너는 걸어서 건널 수 있어.

306	**costume** [kɑ́stjuːm]	몧 의상, 복장

- The hanbok is the Korean traditional **costume**. 한복은 한국의 전통 의상이다.
- Sam wore ghost _____s on Halloween. Sam은 핼러윈 때 유령 복장을 입었다.

307	**throw** [θrou] throw-threw-thrown	통 던지다

- The pitcher **threw** the ball to the catcher. 투수가 포수에게 공을 던졌다.
- _____ the dice to start the game. 게임을 시작하려면 주사위를 던지세요.

308	**opinion** [əpínjən]	몧 의견

- What is your **opinion** on social media? 소셜 미디어에 대한 네 의견은 무엇이니?
- In my _____, Alice is very smart. 내 생각에 Alice는 매우 똑똑하다.

309	**result** [rizʌ́lt]	몧 결과 통 (~의 결과로) 발생하다

- I wasn't happy with the test **result**. 나는 시험 결과에 만족하지 못했다.
- Mr. Hill's success _____ed from his hard work. Hill 씨의 성공은 열심히 일한 결과였다.

310	**switch** [switʃ]	몧 스위치 통 (하던 일·사용하던 것 등을) 바꾸다, 전환하다

- Which **switch** is for the light? 어느 스위치가 전등용인가요?
- This TV show is boring. Let's _____ the channel. 이 TV 쇼는 지루해. 채널을 돌리자.

311	**anxious**	웹 걱정하는, 간절히 원하는		anxiety 명 걱정, 근심

311

anxious
[ǽŋkʃəs]

형 걱정하는, 간절히 원하는　　　　　　　　　　　　anxiety 명 걱정, 근심

- Mr. Scott is **anxious** about losing his hair. Scott 씨는 탈모를 걱정하고 있다.
- I was ＿＿＿＿ to know my test score. 나는 시험 점수를 알기를 원했다.

312

continue
[kəntínju(:)]

동 (쉬지 않고) 계속하다, 지속되다

- The rain **continued** to fall today. 오늘은 비가 계속 내렸다.
- How long will this sale ＿＿＿＿? 이 세일은 언제까지 계속되나요?

313

emotion
[imóuʃən]

명 감정　　　　　　　　　　　　　　　　　emotional 형 감정의, 감정적인

- We cannot always control our **emotions**. 우리가 감정을 항상 통제할 수 있는 것은 아니다.
- We can express ＿＿＿＿s through gestures. 우리는 몸짓을 통해서 감정을 표현할 수 있다.

314

notice
[nóutis]

동 (보거나 듣고) 알아차리다　　명 안내, 예고

- Nobody **noticed** my new hairstyle. 아무도 나의 새 헤어스타일을 알아차리지 못했다.
- The event was canceled without any ＿＿＿＿. 그 행사는 예고 없이 취소되었다.

315

silly
[síli]

형 어리석은/바보 같은, 우스꽝스러운

- I won't answer such a **silly** question. 나는 그처럼 어리석은 질문에는 대답하지 않을 거야.
- You look ＿＿＿＿ in those huge boots. 너는 그 커다란 부츠를 신으니 우스꽝스러워 보여.

Check Up

A 다음 영어단어를 듣고 해당 번호를 쓰시오. 그 다음, 빈칸에 우리말을 쓰시오. 🎧53

opinion ☐	toward ☐	public ☐	switch ☐
＿＿＿＿	＿＿＿＿	＿＿＿＿	＿＿＿＿
continue ☐	anxious ☐	result ☐	notice ☐
＿＿＿＿	＿＿＿＿	＿＿＿＿	＿＿＿＿

B 다음 우리말에 해당하는 영어단어를 쓰시오.

1 개울　＿＿＿＿＿＿＿　　2 감정　＿＿＿＿＿＿＿

3 농담　＿＿＿＿＿＿＿　　4 접다　＿＿＿＿＿＿＿

5 던지다　＿＿＿＿＿＿＿　　6 의상　＿＿＿＿＿＿＿

7 어리석은　＿＿＿＿＿＿＿

54

316	**lead**	⑧ 이끌다, ~으로 이어지다/연결되다
	[li:d]	• The tour guide **led** us to the museum. 여행 가이드는 우리를 박물관으로 안내했다.
	lead-led-led	• This road _____s to the shopping area. 이 도로는 상가 지역으로 이어진다.

317	**recipe**	⑲ 요리법, 레시피
	[résəpì:]	• Can you give me the **recipe** for the soup? 그 수프 요리법을 알려줄 수 있니?
		• Make a cake according to the _____. 그 요리법에 따라 케이크를 만드세요.

318	**trade**	⑲ 거래, 무역 ⑧ 거래하다
	[treid]	• Korea does a lot of **trade** with the U.S. 한국은 미국과 많은 무역을 한다.
		• The company _____s their products mostly in Europe. 그 회사는 주로 유럽에서 상품들을 거래한다.

319	**hammer**	⑲ 망치
	[hǽmər]	• There are two **hammers** in the toolbox. 도구 상자에 두 개의 망치가 있다.
		• Use the _____ to drive the nails. 망치를 사용해서 못을 박으세요.

320	**thick**	⑲ 두꺼운
	[θik]	• This book is too **thick** to hold with one hand. 이 책은 너무 두꺼워서 한 손으로 잡을 수가 없어.
		• The girl was wearing _____ glasses. 그 여자아이는 두꺼운 안경을 쓰고 있었다.

321	**courage**	⑲ 용기
	[kə́:ridʒ]	• Warriors must have great **courage**. 전사들은 큰 용기를 가지고 있어야 한다.
		• I didn't have the _____ to say "no." 나는 "아니오"라고 말할 용기가 나지 않았다.

322	**interesting**	⑲ 흥미로운 interested ⑲흥미가 있는 interest ⑧~의 관심을 끌다 ⑲관심, 흥미
	[íntərəstiŋ]	• The novel is **interesting**. I read it several times. 그 소설은 흥미로워. 나는 여러 번 읽었어.
		• It is always _____ to go to new places. 새로운 곳에 가는 것은 항상 흥미롭다.

323	**ordinary**	⑲ 보통의, 일상적인
	[ɔ́:rdənèri]	• Van Gogh painted mostly **ordinary** people. 반 고흐는 주로 평범한 사람들을 그렸다.
		• It is just an _____ day. 그저 일상적인 날이야.

324	**review**	⑧ 검토하다, 복습하다 ⑲ 검토, (책·영화·상품 등에 대한) 평가/리뷰
	[rivjú:]	• **Review** the contract before you sign it. 서명을 하기 전에 계약서를 검토하세요.
		• Jamie wrote a book _____ on his blog. Jamie는 자신의 블로그에 책 리뷰를 썼다.

325	**symbol**	⑲ 상징, 기호
	[símbəl]	• The eagle was the **symbol** of ancient Rome. 독수리는 고대 로마의 상징이었다.
		• Do you know what this _____ means? 너는 이 기호가 무엇을 의미하는지 아니?

326 apologize
[əpάlədʒàiz]

⟨동⟩ 사과하다

apology ⟨명⟩ 사과

- I **apologize** if I made you feel bad. 제가 기분을 상하게 했다면 죄송해요.
- Taylor _____ d to us for being late. Taylor는 늦은 것에 대해 우리에게 사과했다.

---

327 creature
[krí:tʃər]

⟨명⟩ 생물, 생명체

- What is the biggest **creature** on Earth? 지구에서 가장 큰 생물은 무엇이니?
- _____ s cannot live without water. 생명체는 물 없이 살 수 없다.

---

328 equipment
[ikwípmənt]

⟨명⟩ 장비

- The laboratory has some expensive **equipment**. 그 실험실에는 값비싼 장비들이 있다.
- You need special _____ to scuba dive. 스쿠버 다이빙을 하려면 특별한 장비가 필요하다.

---

329 offer
[ɔ́(:)fər]

⟨동⟩ (기회·도움 등을) 제안하다 ⟨명⟩ 제안

- Jacob **offered** to help me with the homework. Jacob이 내 숙제를 도와 주겠다고 제안했다.
- I refused his _____ of ice cream. 나는 아이스크림을 주겠다는 그의 제안을 거절했다.

---

330 similar
[símələr]

⟨형⟩ 비슷한, 유사한

- Lauren's hairstyle is **similar** to mine. Lauren의 헤어스타일은 나와 비슷하다.
- My sister and I don't look _____ at all. 언니와 나는 전혀 닮지 않았다.

Check Up

정답 p.122

A 다음 영어단어를 듣고 해당 번호를 쓰시오. 그 다음, 빈칸에 우리말을 쓰시오. ◖55◗

similar ☐	hammer ☐	equipment ☐	symbol ☐
___	___	___	___
courage ☐	creature ☐	trade ☐	interesting ☐
___	___	___	___

B 다음 우리말에 해당하는 영어단어를 쓰시오.

1 사과하다 _____   2 이끌다 _____

3 제안하다 _____   4 보통의 _____

5 두꺼운 _____   6 요리법 _____

7 검토하다 _____

A 다음 영어단어의 우리말을 쓰시오.

1 throw _____ 2 recipe _____

3 stream _____ 4 anxious _____

5 costume _____ 6 interesting _____

7 public _____ 8 lead _____

9 equipment _____ 10 offer _____

11 opinion _____ 12 apologize _____

B 우리말과 일치하도록 알맞은 영어단어를 써넣어 문장을 완성하시오.

1 The eagle was the _____ of ancient Rome. 독수리는 고대 로마의 <u>상징</u>이었다.

2 We can express _____s through gestures. 우리는 몸짓을 통해서 <u>감정</u>을 표현할 수 있다.

3 Warriors must have great _____. 전사들은 큰 <u>용기</u>를 가지고 있어야 한다.

4 I wasn't happy with the test _____. 나는 시험 <u>결과</u>에 만족하지 못했다.

5 Everybody laughed at my _____. 내 <u>농담</u>에 모든 사람들이 웃었다.

6 My sister and I don't look _____ at all. 언니와 나는 전혀 <u>닮지</u> 않았다.

7 Use the _____ to drive the nails. <u>망치</u>를 사용해서 못을 박으세요.

8 The girl was wearing _____ glasses. 그 여자아이는 <u>두꺼운</u> 안경을 쓰고 있었다.

9 Let's _____ the colored paper into a ball. 색종이를 <u>접어서</u> 공을 만들자.

10 _____ the contract before you sign it. 서명을 하기 전에 계약서를 <u>검토하세요</u>.

C 다음 영어문장이 우리말과 일치하면 O, 그렇지 않으면 X를 쓰시오.

1 You look ordinary in those huge boots. 너는 그 커다란 부츠를 신으니 우스꽝스러워 보여. (   )

2 The rain continued to fall today. 오늘은 비가 계속 내렸다. (   )

3 Visitors are walking toward the lobby. 방문객들이 로비 쪽으로 걸어가고 있다. (   )

4 What is the biggest creature on Earth? 지구에서 가장 큰 생물은 무엇이니? (   )

5 The event was canceled without any switch. 그 행사는 예고 없이 취소되었다. (   )

D 다음 문장을 듣고 문장을 완성한 후, 빈칸에 쓴 영어단어의 우리말을 쓰시오. 🎧56

1 Mr. Baker made some _____s before his speech.
➡ ....

2 What is your _____ on social media?
➡ ....

3 _____s cannot live without water.
➡ ....

4 Can you give me the _____ for the soup?
➡ ....

5 The _____ is quite shallow. You can walk across it.
➡ ....

6 I won't answer such a _____ question.
➡ ....

7 Lauren's hairstyle is _____ to mine.
➡ ....

8 Mr. Hill's success _____ed from his hard work.
➡ ....

9 This road _____s to the shopping area.
➡ ....

10 I refused his _____ of ice cream.
➡ ....

11 Sam wore ghost _____s on Halloween.
➡ ....

12 The laboratory has some expensive _____.
➡ ....

13 Mr. Scott is _____ about losing his hair.
➡ ....

14 Korea does a lot of _____ with the U.S.
➡ ....

15 This TV show is boring. Let's _____ the channel.
➡ ....

16 _____ the dice to start the game.
➡ ....

17 Van Gogh painted mostly _____ people.
➡ ....

18 _____ your T-shirts and put them in the drawer.
➡ ....

19 There are two _____s in the toolbox.
➡ ....

20 Do you know what this _____ means?
➡ ....

21 I _____ if I made you feel bad.
➡ ....

22 How long will this sale _____?
➡ ....

23 This book is too _____ to hold with one hand.
➡ ....

24 We cannot always control our _____s,
➡ ....

25 Most plants grow _____ the sunlight.
➡ ....

26 I didn't have the _____ to say "no."
➡ ....

27 Jamie wrote a book _____ on his blog.
➡ ....

28 The novel is _____. I read it several times.
➡ ....

29 Nobody _____d my new hairstyle.
➡ ....

30 We can use the _____ library for free.
➡ ....

331	**level** [lévəl]	몧 수준, 단계

- My Spanish **level** is not very high. 내 스페인어 수준은 그다지 높지 않다.
- I want to improve my _____ of basketball. 내 농구 실력을 향상시키고 싶어.

332	**record** [rékərd]	몧 (글 등으로 남긴) 기록, (스포츠에서의) 기록 동 기록하다 [rikɔ́ːrd]

- The athlete broke the world **record**. 그 선수가 세계 기록을 경신했다.
- The doctor _____ed the patient's symptoms. 의사는 환자의 증상을 기록했다.

333	**trick** [trik]	몧 속임수, 장난 동 속이다

- My brother often plays **tricks** on me. 우리 형은 나에게 자주 장난을 친다.
- Kevin tried to _____ me by telling a lie. Kevin은 거짓말로 나를 속이려고 했다.

334	**harvest** [háːrvist]	몧 수확 (시기), 수확량 동 거두다, 수확하다

- We had a poor **harvest** because of the drought. 가뭄 때문에 수확량이 좋지 못했다.
- Some farmers are _____ing their fields. 몇몇 농부들이 들판에서 수확을 하고 있다.

335	**though** [ðou]	접 ~이지만 부 그러나, 하지만

- Leah failed the exam **though** she worked hard. 열심히 공부했지만 Leah는 시험에 떨어졌다.
- Julie likes singing. She is not a good singer _____.
  Julie는 노래 부르는 걸 좋아해. 잘하지는 못하지만 말이야.

336	**dictionary** [díkʃənèri]	몧 사전

- A **dictionary** shows the meaning of a word. 사전은 단어의 의미를 보여 준다.
- A _____ lists words in alphabetical order. 사전은 알파벳 순서로 단어들을 나열한다.

337	**international** [ìntərnǽʃənəl]	혱 국제적인

- The United Nations is an **international** organization. 국제 연합(UN)은 국제적인 단체이다.
- My brother has an _____ driver's license. 우리 형은 국제 면허증이 있다.

338	**pain** [pein]	몧 통증, 고통 painful 혱 아픈, 고통스러운

- Because of the **pain** in my tooth, I went to a dentist. 나는 이가 아파서 치과에 갔다.
- We want to live a life without _____. 우리는 고통 없이 살기를 원한다.

339	**roll** [roul]	동 구르다, 굴러가다

- A huge rock is **rolling** down the hill. 커다란 바위가 언덕 아래로 굴러가고 있다.
- Some coins _____ed under the sofa. 동전 몇 개가 소파 아래로 굴러 들어갔다.

340	**task** [tæsk]	몧 일, 업무

- I need more time to complete the **task**. 나는 그 일을 끝내기 위해서 시간이 더 필요하다.
- This _____ is difficult for middle school students. 이 일은 중학생에게는 어렵다.

341 **arrest**

[ərést]

(동) 체포하다

• The police officers **arrested** the man for stealing a car.
경찰관들은 차를 훔쳤다는 이유로 그 남자를 체포했다.

• The thief was ⬚⬚⬚⬚⬚ed and put into jail. 그 도둑은 체포되어 감옥에 보내졌다.

342 **curl**

[kə:rl]

(동) 곱슬거리게 하다, 동그랗게 말리게 하다   (명) 곱슬곱슬한 머리카락

• My mom always **curls** her hair. 엄마는 항상 머리를 곱슬곱슬하게 하신다.

• The girl has long brown ⬚⬚⬚⬚⬚s. 그 여자아이는 긴 갈색 곱슬머리를 가졌다.

343 **excellent**

[éksələnt]

(형) 뛰어난, 훌륭한

• Mr. Rooney was an **excellent** soccer player. Rooney 씨는 훌륭한 축구 선수였다.

• The restaurant is famous for its ⬚⬚⬚⬚⬚ service. 그 식당은 뛰어난 서비스로 유명하다.

344 **serve**

[sə:rv]

(동) (식당에서 음식 등을) 제공하다/내오다, 시중들다   service (명) 서비스

• The restaurant **serves** traditional Korean food. 그 식당은 전통 한식을 제공한다.

• The waiter is ⬚⬚⬚⬚⬚ing the customer. 종업원이 고객의 시중을 들고 있다.

345 **situation**

[sìtʃuéiʃən]

(명) 상황

• The **situation** is getting worse and worse. 상황이 점점 악화되고 있다.

• If I were in your ⬚⬚⬚⬚⬚, I would ask for help.
내가 너의 상황이라면, 나는 도움을 요청할 텐데.

Check Up

정답 p.122

A 다음 영어단어를 듣고 해당 번호를 쓰시오. 그 다음, 빈칸에 우리말을 쓰시오. 🎧58

excellent ☐	situation ☐	serve ☐	arrest ☐
_____	_____	_____	_____
international ☐	though ☐	harvest ☐	record ☐
_____	_____	_____	_____

B 다음 우리말에 해당하는 영어단어를 쓰시오.

1 수준 _____   2 구르다 _____

3 곱슬거리게 하다 _____   4 일, 업무 _____

5 속임수 _____   6 통증 _____

7 사전 _____

346	**lift** [lift]	(동) 들어 올리다

- I can't **lift** this box. It's too heavy. 나는 이 상자를 들 수가 없어. 너무 무거워.
- Can you help me ⬚⬚⬚ this sofa? 이 소파 드는 것 좀 도와 줄래?

347	**report** [ripɔ́ːrt]	(동) 알리다, 보도하다, 보고하다　(명) 보고(서)

- The news **reported** that a big fire broke out yesterday.
  뉴스는 어제 큰 화재가 발생했다고 보도했다.
- I'm writing a ⬚⬚⬚ about dolphins. 나는 돌고래에 관한 보고서를 쓰고 있다.

348	**twin** [twin]	(명) 쌍둥이　(형) 쌍둥이의

- The **twins** look very similar. 그 쌍둥이는 매우 닮았다.
- I have a ⬚⬚⬚ brother. 나에게는 쌍둥이 오빠가 있다.

349	**highway** [háiwèi]	(명) 고속도로

- Traffic jams often occur on the **highway**. 그 고속도로는 자주 막힌다.
- The ⬚⬚⬚ connects Seoul and Busan. 그 고속도로는 서울과 부산을 잇는다.

350	**thumb** [θʌm]	(명) 엄지손가락

- The baby is sucking his **thumb**. 아기가 엄지손가락을 빨고 있다.
- I slammed my ⬚⬚⬚ in the door. 나는 문에 엄지손가락을 찧었다.

351	**create** [kriéit]	(동) (없던 것을) 만들어 내다　　　creative (형) 창의적인

- God **created** the world. 신이 세상을 창조했다.
- An artist is ⬚⬚⬚ing a sculpture. 한 예술가가 조각상을 만들고 있다.

352	**pile** [pail]	(명) 쌓아 놓은 것, 더미

- There is a **pile** of papers on the desk. 책상에 종이들이 쌓여 있다.
- They left the towels in a ⬚⬚⬚ on the floor. 그들은 수건을 바닥에 쌓아 놓았다.

353	**palm** [pɑːm]	(명) 손바닥

- The dog put its foot on my **palm**. 그 개는 내 손바닥에 발을 올려 놓았다.
- He wrote down something on his ⬚⬚⬚. 그는 자신의 손바닥에 무언가를 적었다.

354	**royal** [rɔ́iəl]	(형) 국왕의, 왕족의

- We watched the **royal** wedding on TV. 우리는 왕가의 결혼식을 TV로 시청했다.
- The king and queen lived in the ⬚⬚⬚ palace. 그 왕과 왕비는 왕궁에서 살았다.

355	**tear** [tiər] tear-tore-torn	(명) 눈물　(동) 찢다 [tɛər]

- Why were his eyes filled with **tears**? 왜 그의 눈이 눈물로 그렁그렁해졌니?
- ⬚⬚⬚ the paper into two pieces. 그 종이를 두 조각으로 찢어라.

356 **athlete**
[ǽθliːt]

명 운동선수

• Thousands of **athletes** compete in the Olympic Games.
수천 명의 운동선수들이 올림픽에서 경쟁한다.

• A good   needs a good coach. 훌륭한 운동선수는 훌륭한 코치를 필요로 한다.

---

357 **decision**
[disíʒən]

명 결정   decide 동 결정하다

• We should make a **decision** quickly. 우리는 빨리 결정을 내려야 해.

• Who didn't agree with the   ? 누가 그 결정에 반대했니?

---

358 **except**
[iksépt]

전 ~을 제외하고

• Everyone is here **except** Aaron. Aaron을 제외하고는 모든 사람이 왔다.

• The library is open daily   Mondays. 그 도서관은 월요일만 빼고 매일 문을 연다.

---

359 **pace**
[peis]

명 (걸음 등의) 속도

• Karl walks at a fast **pace**. Karl은 빠른 속도로 걷는다.

• The   of the parade was slow. 행진의 속도는 느렸다.

---

360 **skip**
[skip]

동 (일을) 거르다/빼먹다

• My sister often **skips** breakfast. 우리 언니는 자주 아침 식사를 거른다.

• I want to   my piano lesson today. 저는 오늘 피아노 수업을 빠지고 싶어요.

Check Up

정답 p.123

A 다음 영어단어를 듣고 해당 번호를 쓰시오. 그 다음, 빈칸에 우리말을 쓰시오. 🎧60

decision	☐	pile	☐	create	☐	athlete	☐
_____		_____		_____		_____	

palm	☐	highway	☐	royal	☐	thumb	☐
_____		_____		_____		_____	

B 다음 우리말에 해당하는 영어단어를 쓰시오.

1 눈물   _____   2 ~을 제외하고   _____

3 쌍둥이   _____   4 들어 올리다   _____

5 (걸음 등의) 속도   _____   6 (일을) 거르다   _____

7 알리다   _____

정답 p.123

A 다음 영어단어의 우리말을 쓰시오.

1 dictionary _____   2 level _____

3 highway _____   4 arrest _____

5 situation _____   6 international _____

7 pile _____   8 palm _____

9 task _____   10 except _____

11 royal _____   12 athlete _____

B 우리말과 일치하도록 알맞은 영어단어를 써넣어 문장을 완성하시오.

1 The athlete broke the world _____. 그 선수가 세계 기록을 경신했다.

2 Who didn't agree with the _____? 누가 그 결정에 반대했니?

3 Karl walks at a fast _____. Karl은 빠른 속도로 걷는다.

4 Can you help me _____ this sofa? 이 소파 드는 것 좀 도와 줄래?

5 Mr. Rooney was an _____ soccer player. Rooney 씨는 뛰어난 축구 선수였다.

6 The _____s look very similar. 그 쌍둥이는 매우 닮았다.

7 We want to live a life without _____. 우리는 고통없이 살기를 원한다.

8 The baby is sucking his _____. 아기가 엄지손가락을 빨고 있다.

9 My sister often _____s breakfast. 우리 언니는 자주 아침 식사를 거른다.

10 A huge rock is _____ing down the hill. 커다란 바위가 언덕 아래로 굴러가고 있다.

C 다음 영어문장이 우리말과 일치하면 O, 그렇지 않으면 X를 쓰시오.

1 My mom always curls her hair. 엄마는 항상 머리를 곱슬곱슬하게 하신다. (   )

2 We had a poor trick because of the drought. 가뭄 때문에 수확량이 좋지 못했다. (   )

3 Tear the paper into two pieces. 종이를 두 조각으로 찢어라. (   )

4 An artist is reporting a sculpture. 한 예술가가 조각상을 만들고 있다. (   )

5 The waiter is serving the customer. 종업원이 고객의 시중을 들고 있다. (   )

D 다음 문장을 듣고 문장을 완성한 후, 빈칸에 쓴 영어단어의 우리말을 쓰시오. 🎧 61

1 I want to _____ my piano lesson today. → ....

2 We watched the _____ wedding on TV. → ....

3 The _____ is getting worse and worse. → ....

4 I want to improve my _____ of basketball. → ....

5 The thief was _____ed and put into jail. → ....

6 They left the towels in a _____ on the floor. → ....

7 I need more time to complete the _____. → ....

8 God _____d the world. → ....

9 The restaurant _____s traditional Korean food. → ....

10 Why were his eyes filled with _____s? → ....

11 The _____ connects Seoul and Busan. → ....

12 The girl has long brown _____s. → ....

13 Some coins _____ed under the sofa. → ....

14 The dog put its foot on my _____. → ....

15 The _____ of the parade was slow. → ....

16 I slammed my _____ in the door. → ....

17 The restaurant is famous for its _____ service. → ....

18 A good _____ needs a good coach. → ....

19 I can't _____ this box. It's too heavy. → ....

20 Leah failed the exam _____ she worked hard. → ....

21 The United Nations is an _____ organization. → ....

22 The doctor _____ed the patient's symptoms. → ....

23 We should make a _____ quickly. → ....

24 A _____ shows the meaning of a word. → ....

25 Because of the _____ in my tooth, I went to a dentist. → ....

26 I'm writing a _____ about dolphins. → ....

27 Kevin tried to _____ me by telling a lie. → ....

28 I have a _____ brother. → ....

29 Some farmers are _____ing their fields. → ....

30 Everyone is here _____ Aaron. → ....

361 list
[list]

명 목록, 명단

• I bought everything on the shopping **list**. 나는 쇼핑 목록에 있는 것을 다 샀다.

• Please check if my name is on the waiting _____.
대기자 명단에 제 이름이 있는지 확인해 주세요.

362 ride
[raid]
ride-rode-ridden

동 (자전거 등을) 직접 몰다/타다, (버스·차 등을) 타고 가다

• A boy is **riding** a bike. 한 남자아이가 자전거를 타고 있다.

• My dad usually _____ s a bus to work. 아빠는 보통 버스를 타고 출근하신다.

363 clinic
[klínik]

명 진료소, 병원

• The doctor opened a free **clinic** for babies. 그 의사는 아기들을 위한 무료 진료소를 열었다.

• Call the dental _____ to make an appointment. 치과에 전화해서 예약을 해라.

364 knight
[nait]

명 기사

• The **knight** had a sword and a shield. 그 기사는 검과 방패를 가지고 있었다.

• The _____ s fought bravely for their king. 그 기사들은 왕을 위해 용감히 싸웠다.

365 toe
[tou]

명 발가락

• Ballerinas can stand on their **toes**. 발레리나는 발가락으로 설 수 있다.

• I broke my _____ during a soccer game. 나는 축구 시합 중에 발가락 하나가 부러졌다.

366 deliver
[dilívər]

동 배달하다   delivery 명 배달

• Your sofa will be **delivered** tomorrow. 당신의 소파는 내일 배달될 것입니다.

• A mailman is _____ ing mail. 집배원이 우편물을 배달하고 있다.

367 journal
[dʒə́:rnəl]

명 일기, 잡지

• I keep a **journal** every day. 나는 매일 일기를 쓴다.

• The paper was published in a scientific _____. 그 논문은 과학 잡지에 발표되었다.

368 peel
[pi:l]

동 (과일·채소 등의) 껍질을 벗기다   명 껍질

• Emma is **peeling** some potatoes in the kitchen. Emma는 부엌에서 감자 껍질을 벗기고 있다.

• Remove the _____ before you eat the pear. 배를 먹기 전에 껍질을 벗겨라.

369 rude
[ru:d]

형 무례한, 버릇없는

• It is **rude** to keep others waiting. 다른 사람들을 기다리게 하는 것은 무례한 행동이다.

• I was angry at the kid's _____ behavior. 나는 그 아이의 버릇없는 행동에 화가 났다.

370 temperature
[témpərətʃər]

명 온도

• The **temperature** of the desert is very high. 사막의 온도는 매우 높다.

• A nurse is taking the man's body _____. 간호사가 남자의 체온을 재고 있다.

371 **attend**
[əténd]

동 참석하다, (학교·교회 등에) 다니다

• Many people will **attend** the festival. 많은 사람들이 그 축제에 참석할 것이다.
• Children _____ elementary schools at the age of eight.
아이들은 8세가 되면 초등학교에 다닌다.

372 **decorate**
[dékərèit]

동 장식하다, 꾸미다   decoration 명 장식

• We **decorated** the Christmas tree with ribbons. 우리는 리본으로 크리스마스트리를 장식했다.
• Alex _____ d the cake with strawberries. Alex는 딸기로 케이크를 장식했다.

373 **expensive**
[ikspénsiv]

형 비싼

• This computer is more **expensive** than that one. 이 컴퓨터는 저 컴퓨터보다 비싸다.
• The watch is too _____ to buy. 그 시계는 너무 비싸서 살 수가 없다.

374 **pack**
[pæk]

동 (짐을) 싸다

• Can you help me **pack** the suitcase? 여행 가방 싸는 것을 좀 도와 줄래?
• I forgot to _____ my camera. 나는 카메라 챙기는 것을 잊었어.

375 **spot**
[spɑt]

명 반점, 얼룩, 장소

• The dog has black **spots** on its back. 그 개는 등에 검은 반점들이 있다.
• Bali is a popular vacation _____. 발리는 인기 있는 휴가지이다.

Check Up

정답 p.123

A 다음 영어단어를 듣고 해당 번호를 쓰시오. 그 다음, 빈칸에 우리말을 쓰시오. 🎧63

peel ☐	expensive ☐	ride ☐	decorate ☐

temperature ☐	deliver ☐	journal ☐	attend ☐

B 다음 우리말에 해당하는 영어단어를 쓰시오.

1 발가락 _____   2 반점 _____

3 무례한 _____   4 진료소, 병원 _____

5 목록 _____   6 (짐을) 싸다 _____

7 기사 _____

64

---

376 **loud**
[laud]

형 시끄러운, 소리가 큰

- My next door neighbor made **loud** noises yesterday. 어제 옆집에서 시끄러운 소리가 났다.
- A child is crying in a   voice. 한 아이가 큰 소리로 울고 있다.

---

377 **rope**
[roup]

명 밧줄

- Some sailors are pulling the **rope**. 몇 명의 선원들이 밧줄을 잡아당기고 있다.
- The mouse cut the   with its teeth. 그 생쥐는 이빨로 밧줄을 끊었다.

---

378 **view**
[vju:]

명 생각/의견, 전망

- I have a different **view** from you. 나는 너와 다른 생각을 가지고 있어.
- I stayed at the hotel room with an ocean   . 나는 바다 전망의 호텔 객실에 묵었다.

---

379 **knock**
[nɑk]

동 (문 등을) 두드리다, 노크하다

- **Knock** on the door before you come in. 들어오기 전에 문을 두드리세요.
- Someone   ed on the window. 누군가가 창문을 두드렸다.

---

380 **tool**
[tu:l]

명 도구

- The mechanic used some **tools** to fix the car. 정비사는 몇 가지 도구를 사용하여 차를 고쳤다.
- Handle the   s carefully. 도구들을 조심히 다루세요.

---

381 **determine**
[ditə́:rmin]

동 결정하다

- Each school **determines** its school uniform. 각 학교마다 교복을 결정한다.
- We were   d to change some of the rules. 우리는 일부 규칙을 바꾸기로 결정했다.

---

382 **judge**
[dʒʌdʒ]

명 판사, 심사위원   동 판단하다

- **Judges** should always be fair. 판사는 항상 공정해야 한다.
- Don't   a man by his appearance. 외모로 사람을 판단하지 마세요.

---

383 **perfect**
[pə́:rfikt]

형 완벽한, 가장 좋은

- The pianist's performance was **perfect**. 그 피아노 연주자의 연주는 완벽했다.
- Fall is the   time to read books. 가을은 독서를 하기에 가장 좋은 시기이다.

---

384 **scare**
[skɛər]

동 겁을 주다, 무섭게 만들다   scary 형 무서운, 겁나는

- Ghosts can't **scare** me. 나는 유령이 겁나지 않아.
- The horror story   d all of us. 그 공포 이야기는 우리 모두를 무섭게 했다.

---

385 **benefit**
[bénəfit]

명 이로운 점

- What is the **benefit** of reading books? 독서의 이점이 무엇이니?
- Yoga brings many health   s. 요가는 건강상 많은 이점이 있다.

---

386 available

[əvéiləbl]

형 이용 가능한, 구할 수 있는

- Delivery service is not **available** now. 현재 배달 서비스는 이용하실 수 없습니다.
- Do you have a room   today? 오늘 이용 가능한 객실이 있나요?

387 delight

[diláit]

명 기쁨 동 기쁨을 주다

delighted 형 기쁜

- The woman received the gift with **delight**. 그 여자는 기뻐하며 선물을 받았다.
- Jack   ed us with the chocolate cake. Jack은 초콜릿 케이크로 우리를 기쁘게 했다.

388 expert

[ékspəːrt]

명 전문가

- My dad is an **expert** at camping. 우리 아빠는 캠핑 전문가이시다.
- Most   s expected the German soccer team to win.
  대부분의 전문가들은 독일 축구 팀이 이길 것으로 예상했다.

389 panic

[pǽnik]

panic-panicked-
panicked

명 (갑작스러운) 극도의 공포 동 (놀라서) 어쩔 줄 모르게 하다

- The fire caused a **panic** in the building. 화재로 건물 안이 공황 상태가 되었다.
- The terrible news   ked us. 그 끔찍한 소식 때문에 우리는 어쩔 줄 몰랐다.

390 steam

[stiːm]

명 증기, 김

- **Steam** is coming out of the kettle. 주전자에서 김이 나오고 있다.
- The first engine was powered by   . 최초의 엔진은 증기로 작동되었다.

Check Up

정답 p.123

A 다음 영어단어를 듣고 해당 번호를 쓰시오. 그 다음, 빈칸에 우리말을 쓰시오. 🎧65

view	☐	judge	☐	knock	☐	benefit	☐
_____		_____		_____		_____	
determine	☐	available	☐	delight	☐	panic	☐
_____		_____		_____		_____	

B 다음 우리말에 해당하는 영어단어를 쓰시오.

1 밧줄   _____   2 겁을 주다   _____

3 전문가   _____   4 시끄러운   _____

5 증기   _____   6 완벽한   _____

7 도구   _____

A 다음 영어단어의 우리말을 쓰시오.

1 knight _____

2 determine _____

3 journal _____

4 pack _____

5 scare _____

6 perfect _____

7 expert _____

8 temperature _____

9 loud _____

10 delight _____

11 clinic _____

12 list _____

B 우리말과 일치하도록 알맞은 영어단어를 써넣어 문장을 완성하시오.

1 The first engine was powered by _____ . 최초의 엔진은 증기로 작동되었다.

2 Your sofa will be _____ed tomorrow. 당신의 소파는 내일 배달될 것입니다.

3 It is _____ to keep others waiting. 다른 사람을 기다리게 하는 것은 무례한 행동이다.

4 Ballerinas can stand on their _____s. 발레리나는 발가락으로 설 수 있다.

5 The watch is too _____ to buy. 그 시계는 너무 비싸서 살 수가 없다.

6 _____s should always be fair. 판사는 항상 공정해야 한다.

7 Handle the _____s carefully. 도구들을 조심히 다루세요.

8 Many people will _____ the festival. 많은 사람들이 그 축제에 참석할 것이다.

9 Some sailors are pulling the _____ . 몇 명의 선원들이 밧줄을 잡아당기고 있다.

10 Someone _____ed on the window. 누군가가 창문을 두드렸다.

C 다음 영어문장이 우리말과 일치하면 O, 그렇지 않으면 X를 쓰시오.

1 Emma is panicking some potatoes in the kitchen. Emma는 부엌에서 감자 껍질을 벗기고 있다. ( )

2 I have a different spot from you. 나는 너와 다른 생각을 가지고 있어. ( )

3 Delivery service is not available now. 현재 배달 서비스는 이용하실 수 없습니다. ( )

4 Yoga brings many health benefits. 요가는 건강에 많은 이로운 점을 준다. ( )

5 A boy is decorating a bike. 한 소년이 자전거를 타고 있다. ( )

D 다음 문장을 듣고 문장을 완성한 후, 빈칸에 쓴 영어단어의 우리말을 쓰시오. 🎧66

1 _____ is coming out of the kettle. ➡ ....

2 Do you have a room _____ today? ➡ ....

3 Children _____ elementary schools at the age of eight. ➡ ....

4 _____ on the door before you come in. ➡ ....

5 The horror story _____d all of us. ➡ ....

6 Remove the _____ before you eat the pear. ➡ ....

7 The mechanic used some _____s to fix the car. ➡ ....

8 We _____d the Christmas tree with ribbons. ➡ ....

9 The _____ of the desert is very high. ➡ ....

10 The woman received the gift with _____. ➡ ....

11 I was angry at the kid's _____ behavior. ➡ ....

12 This computer is more _____ than that one. ➡ ....

13 I stayed at the hotel room with an ocean _____. ➡ ....

14 I keep a _____ every day. ➡ ....

15 The fire caused a _____ in the building. ➡ ....

16 A mailman is _____ing mail. ➡ ....

17 Each school _____s its school uniform. ➡ ....

18 Can you help me _____ the suitcase? ➡ ....

19 My dad usually _____s a bus to work. ➡ ....

20 The pianist's performance was _____. ➡ ....

21 Call the dental _____ to make an appointment. ➡ ....

22 I broke my _____ during a soccer game. ➡ ....

23 What is the _____ of reading books? ➡ ....

24 The mouse cut the _____ with its teeth. ➡ ....

25 I bought everything on the shopping _____. ➡ ....

26 My next door neighbor made _____ noises yesterday. ➡ ....

27 Don't _____ a man by his appearance. ➡ ....

28 The _____ had a sword and a shield. ➡ ....

29 The dog has black _____s on its back. ➡ ....

30 My dad is an _____ at camping. ➡ ....

Lesson

27

67

391 magazine
[mǽgəzíːn]

몡 잡지
- I usually read fashion **magazines**. 나는 주로 패션 잡지를 읽는다.
- The _____ comes out every month. 그 잡지는 매달 출간된다.

392 author
[ɔ́ːθər]

몡 작가
- Who is the **author** of the book? 그 책의 작가가 누구니?
- The _____ wrote many fantasy novels. 그 작가는 많은 판타지 소설을 썼다.

393 village
[vílidʒ]

몡 마을
- My grandfather lives in a small **village**. 우리 할아버지는 작은 마을에 살고 계신다.
- Are there any hotels in this _____? 이 마을에 호텔이 있나요?

394 law
[lɔː]

몡 법
- The man broke the **law** and got arrested. 그 남자는 법을 위반해서 체포되었다.
- By _____, you can't smoke in public places. 법에 따라, 공공장소에서는 흡연할 수 없다.

395 victory
[víktəri]

몡 승리
- The player did his best to get a **victory**. 그 선수는 이기기 위해 최선을 다했다.
- The battle ended in a _____ for us. 그 전투는 우리의 승리로 끝났다.

396 craft
[kræft]

몡 공예, 공예품
- The small town is known for its glass **crafts**. 그 작은 도시는 유리 공예로 유명하다.
- A paper fan is one of the traditional Korean _____s.
종이 부채는 전통적인 한국 공예품 중 하나이다.

397 kingdom
[kíŋdəm]

몡 왕국
- The queen ruled the **kingdom** for 20 years. 그 여왕은 20년 동안 왕국을 지배했다.
- The king wanted to expand his _____. 그 왕은 왕국을 넓히고 싶어 했다.

398 photograph
[fóutəgræf]

몡 사진
- You can't take **photographs** here. 여기서는 사진을 찍으실 수 없습니다.
- I have a _____ of my family in my wallet. 내 지갑 안에는 우리 가족의 사진이 있다.

399 search
[səːrtʃ]

동 (구석구석) 찾다, (인터넷으로) 찾아보다
- The police are **searching** for the missing boy. 경찰들이 실종된 남자아이를 찾고 있다.
- _____ for more information on the Internet. 인터넷으로 더 많은 정보를 찾으세요.

400 throat
[θrout]

몡 목구멍, 목
- I have a sore **throat** and cough. 저는 목이 아프고 기침이 나요.
- The man often cleared his _____. 그 남자는 자주 목을 가다듬었다.

401 average
[ǽvəridʒ]

(형) 평균의, 보통의/일반적인

- What is the **average** temperature here? 이곳의 평균 기온은 얼마인가요?
- The _____ Korean reads nine books a year.
  보통의 한국 사람은 일년에 9권의 책을 읽는다.

402 describe
[diskráib]

(동) 자세히 말하다, 묘사하다

description (명) 묘사

- Can you **describe** the robber? 그 도둑의 인상을 설명해 줄 수 있나요?
- The woman _____d her experience in Sweden.
  그 여자는 스웨덴에서의 자신의 경험을 말해 주었다.

403 explore
[ikspló:r]

(동) 탐사하다, 탐험하다

- The divers are **exploring** the underwater cave. 잠수부들이 수중 동굴을 탐사하고 있다.
- We _____d the Amazon jungle last year. 우리는 작년에 아마존 정글을 탐험했다.

404 particular
[pərtíkjələr]

(형) 특정한

particularly (부) 특별히, 특히

- Max wanted a **particular** type of dog. Max는 특정한 종류의 개를 원했다.
- Is there any _____ item you are looking for? 찾고 있는 특정한 물건이 있나요?

405 stomach
[stʌ́mək]

(명) 위, 복부, 배

- I had a sudden pain in my **stomach**. 나는 갑작스러운 복통이 생겼다.
- My _____ is full. I can't eat any more food. 나는 배가 꽉 찼어. 더 먹지는 못하겠어.

Check Up

정답 p.124

A 다음 영어단어를 듣고 해당 번호를 쓰시오. 그 다음, 빈칸에 우리말을 쓰시오. 🎧 68

| village ☐ | particular ☐ | explore ☐ | throat ☐ |

| kingdom ☐ | describe ☐ | stomach ☐ | photograph ☐ |

B 다음 우리말에 해당하는 영어단어를 쓰시오.

1 법 _____   2 공예 _____

3 작가 _____   4 (구석구석) 찾다 _____

5 평균의 _____   6 승리 _____

7 잡지 _____

95

406	**match** [mætʃ]	동 (물건 등이 서로 잘) 어울리다　명 성냥

- This necklace **matches** your dress. 이 목걸이가 네 드레스와 어울려.
- Use the _____es to light the candle. 성냥을 사용해서 촛불을 켜세요.

407	**seat** [siːt]	명 좌석

- There are four **seats** at the dining table. 그 식탁에는 네 개의 좌석이 있다.
- I was in the front _____ in the theater. 나는 극장에서 맨 앞줄에 앉았다.

408	**weak** [wiːk]	형 (신체적으로) 약한/힘이 없는

- I feel a little **weak** today. 오늘은 좀 기운이 없네요.
- My mom has a _____ stomach. 엄마는 위가 약하시다.

409	**lock** [lɑk]	동 잠그다　명 자물쇠

- Sometimes I forget to **lock** the door. 때때로 나는 문을 잠그는 것을 잊는다.
- Turn the key in the _____ and open the door. 자물쇠에 열쇠를 넣고 돌려 문을 여세요.

410	**within** [wiðín]	전 (특정한 기간·거리) ~ 안에, ~ 이내에

- I'll get there **within** an hour. 나는 한 시간 이내에 그곳에 도착할 거야.
- The building is _____ walking distance. 그 건물은 도보 가능한 거리에 있다.

411	**donate** [dóuneit]	동 기부하다, 기증하다　　donation 명 기부, 기증

- A rich man **donated** 10 million dollars. 어떤 부자가 천만 달러를 기부했다.
- The artist _____d his works to the museum. 그 화가는 박물관에 그의 작품을 기증했다.

412	**language** [læŋgwidʒ]	명 언어

- Austin can speak two foreign **languages**. Austin은 두 개의 외국어를 말할 수 있다.
- Chen's native _____ is Chinese. Chen의 모국어는 중국어이다.

413	**pity** [píti]	명 동정심, 안타까움/유감

- We felt **pity** for the poor dogs. 우리는 불쌍한 개들에게 동정심을 느꼈다.
- It's a _____ that you can't join us. 네가 우리와 함께할 수 없다니 아쉬워.

414	**secret** [síːkrit]	명 비밀

- This is a **secret**. Can you keep it? 이건 비밀이야. 비밀을 지킬 수 있겠니?
- The man was trying to hide his _____. 그 남자는 자신의 비밀을 숨기려고 했다.

415	**inform** [infɔ́ːrm]	동 (정보 등을) 알리다　　information 명 정보

- Please **inform** us of any change in the plan. 계획에 변화가 있다면 저희에게 알려주세요.
- The teacher _____ed us that we would go on a field trip.
  선생님은 우리가 현장체험학습을 갈 거라고 알리셨다.

416 **aware**
[əwɛ́ər]

(형) ~을 알고 있는

- I wasn't **aware** that my mom was sick. 나는 엄마가 아프시다는 것을 모르고 있었다.
- Are you _____ of some cracks in the wall? 너는 벽에 금이 간 것을 알고 있니?

417 **destroy**
[distrɔ́i]

(동) 파괴하다

- The bomb **destroyed** the entire building. 폭탄이 건물 전체를 파괴했다.
- Most of the city was _____ ed by a hurricane.
  도시의 대부분이 허리케인으로 파괴되었다.

418 **fare**
[fɛər]

(명) (교통) 요금

- How much is the subway **fare**? 지하철 요금이 얼마니?
- The ship's _____ to the island is 10 dollars. 그 섬까지의 선박 요금은 10달러이다.

419 **path**
[pæθ]

(명) (사람들이 걸어 다니면서 생긴) 길

- We walked along a narrow **path**. 우리는 좁은 길을 따라 걸었다.
- The forest _____ was covered with fallen leaves. 숲길은 낙엽으로 덮여 있었다.

420 **suddenly**
[sʌ́dnli]

(부) 갑자기, 급작스럽게   sudden (형) 갑작스러운

- **Suddenly**, a strong wind blew. 갑자기 강한 바람이 불었다.
- The field trip was _____ canceled. 현장체험학습이 갑자기 취소되었다.

Check Up

정답 p.124

A 다음 영어단어를 듣고 해당 번호를 쓰시오. 그 다음, 빈칸에 우리말을 쓰시오. 🎧70

destroy ☐	match ☐	donate ☐	inform ☐
_____	_____	_____	_____
path ☐	language ☐	within ☐	aware ☐
_____	_____	_____	_____

B 다음 우리말에 해당하는 영어단어를 쓰시오.

1 (교통) 요금 _____   2 좌석 _____

3 (신체적으로) 약한 _____   4 비밀 _____

5 동정심 _____   6 잠그다 _____

7 갑자기 _____

A 다음 영어단어의 우리말을 쓰시오.

1 particular _____ 2 photograph _____

3 seat _____ 4 weak _____

5 aware _____ 6 destroy _____

7 kingdom _____ 8 explore _____

9 law _____ 10 stomach _____

11 describe _____ 12 search _____

B 우리말과 일치하도록 알맞은 영어단어를 써넣어 문장을 완성하시오.

1 Chen's native _____ is Chinese. Chen의 모국어는 중국어이다.

2 _____, a strong wind blew. 갑자기 강한 바람이 불었다.

3 I usually read fashion _____s. 나는 주로 패션 잡지를 읽는다.

4 The battle ended in a _____ for us. 그 전투는 우리의 승리로 끝났다.

5 This necklace _____es your dress. 이 목걸이가 네 드레스와 어울려.

6 It's a _____ that you can't join us. 네가 우리와 함께할 수 없다니 아쉬워.

7 What is the _____ temperature here? 이곳의 평균 기온은 얼마인가요?

8 A rich man _____d 10 million dollars. 어떤 부자가 천만 달러를 기부했다.

9 This is a _____. Can you keep it? 이건 비밀이야. 비밀을 지킬 수 있겠니?

10 Who is the _____ of the book? 그 책의 작가가 누구니?

C 다음 영어문장이 우리말과 일치하면 O, 그렇지 않으면 X를 쓰시오.

1 I'll get there within an hour. 나는 한 시간 이내에 그곳에 도착할 거야. (   )

2 How much is the subway fare? 지하철 요금이 얼마니? (   )

3 I have a sore throat and cough. 저는 목이 아프고 기침이 나요. (   )

4 Sometimes I forget to inform the door. 때때로 나는 문을 잠그는 것을 잊는다. (   )

5 Are there any hotels in this craft? 이 마을에 호텔이 있나요? (   )

D 다음 문장을 듣고 문장을 완성한 후, 빈칸에 쓴 영어단어의 우리말을 쓰시오. 🎧71

1 The _____ comes out every month. ➔ ....

2 The man broke the _____ and got arrested. ➔ ....

3 The queen ruled the _____ for 20 years. ➔ ....

4 The man was trying to hide his _____. ➔ ....

5 Please _____ us of any change in the plan. ➔ ....

6 Use the _____es to light the candle. ➔ ....

7 The artist _____d his works to the museum. ➔ ....

8 I wasn't _____ that my mom was sick. ➔ ....

9 Austin can speak two foreign _____s. ➔ ....

10 The _____ wrote many fantasy novels. ➔ ....

11 The bomb _____ed the entire building. ➔ ....

12 There are four _____s at the dining table. ➔ ....

13 The field trip was _____ canceled. ➔ ....

14 We felt _____ for the poor dogs. ➔ ....

15 My mom has a _____ stomach. ➔ ....

16 The ship's _____ to the island is 10 dollars. ➔ ....

17 The _____ Korean reads nine books a year. ➔ ....

18 I had a sudden pain in my _____. ➔ ....

19 The building is _____ walking distance. ➔ ....

20 The small town is known for its glass _____s. ➔ ....

21 We walked along a narrow _____. ➔ ....

22 _____ for more information on the Internet. ➔ ....

23 The woman _____d her experience in Sweden. ➔ ....

24 Max wanted a _____ type of dog. ➔ ....

25 My grandfather lives in a small _____. ➔ ....

26 You can't take _____s here. ➔ ....

27 Turn the key in the _____ and open the door. ➔ ....

28 We _____d the Amazon jungle last year. ➔ ....

29 The man often cleared his _____. ➔ ....

30 The player did his best to get a _____. ➔ ....

72

421 probably
[prábəbli]
(부) 아마
- The baby is **probably** sleeping now. 아기는 아마 지금 자고 있을 거야.
- The two people are _____ a couple. 그 두 사람은 아마 부부일 거야.

422 conversation
[kànvərséiʃən]
(명) 대화
- We had a **conversation** about K-pop. 우리는 케이팝에 대해 대화를 나누었다.
- Why don't you join in the _____? 너도 대화에 참여하는 게 어때?

423 whale
[hweil]
(명) 고래
- Some **whales** are swimming in the ocean. 몇몇 고래들이 바다에서 헤엄을 치고 있다.
- _____s and dolphins are mammals. 고래와 돌고래는 포유류이다.

424 mission
[míʃən]
(명) 임무
- I have a **mission** to complete. 나는 끝내야 할 임무가 있어.
- Our _____ is to help the poor children. 우리의 임무는 불쌍한 아이들을 돕는 것이다.

425 package
[pǽkidʒ]
(명) 소포, 꾸러미
- What is in the **package**? 소포 안에 무엇이 들어있니?
- A mailman left a _____ for you. 집배원이 네게 온 소포를 두고 갔어.

426 effect
[ifékt]
(명) 영향, 효과
- Smoking has a bad **effect** on your health. 흡연은 건강에 나쁜 영향을 미친다.
- The medicine had no _____ on me. 그 약은 나에게 효과가 없었다.

427 lay
[lei]
lay-laid-laid
(동) 놓다, 두다
- My dad **laid** his hands on my forehead. 아빠가 내 이마에 손을 올려 놓으셨다.
- Will you _____ the magazine on the table? 그 잡지를 탁자 위에 둘래요?

428 pleasure
[pléʒər]
(명) 기쁨   please (동) 기쁘게 하다   pleasant (형) 기쁜, 즐거운
- It's a **pleasure** to see you again. 당신을 다시 만나게 되어 기쁩니다.
- Traveling always gives me great _____. 여행은 항상 나에게 큰 기쁨을 준다.

429 seem
[si:m]
(동) ~인 것처럼 보이다, ~인 것 같다
- The woman **seemed** tired. 그 여자는 피곤해 보였다.
- Jake _____s like a nice boy. Jake는 착한 소년인 것 같다.

430 tiny
[táini]
(형) 아주 작은
- The glass broke into **tiny** pieces. 유리가 작은 조각들로 깨졌다.
- Can you see that _____ bug over there? 저쪽에 작은 곤충이 보이니?

431 **ban**
[bæn]

ⓈⒹ 금지하다

- The school **banned** using smartphones in class.
  그 학교는 수업 중 학생들의 스마트폰 사용을 금지했다.
- Spitting on the ground is _____ned in Singapore.
  싱가포르에서는 길에 침을 뱉는 것이 금지된다.

432 **direct**
[dirékt]

ⓗ (중간을 거치지 않고) 직접적인, 직행의 ⓈⒹ 지도하다, 감독하다

- I want a **direct** answer from Amy. 나는 Amy에게 직접적인 대답을 듣고 싶어.
- Who _____ed this movie? 누가 이 영화를 감독했나요?

433 **fault**
[fɔːlt]

ⓝ 잘못, 흠

- Don't worry. It's not your **fault**. 걱정하지 마. 네 잘못이 아니야.
- There is no _____ with your essay. 네 과제물에는 잘못된 점이 없어.

434 **patient**
[péiʃənt]

ⓝ 환자 ⓗ 인내심이 있는   patience ⓝ 인내

- A nurse is caring for the old **patient**. 간호사가 나이 많은 환자를 돌보고 있다.
- Be _____ and wait for the result. 인내심을 가지고 결과를 기다려라.

435 **suffer**
[sʌfər]

ⓈⒹ (병 등에) 시달리다, (안 좋은 일을) 겪다

- I **suffered** from a headache last night. 나는 어젯밤에 두통에 시달렸다.
- Japan often _____s damage by earthquakes. 일본은 자주 지진에 의해 피해를 입는다.

Check Up

정답 p.125

Ⓐ 다음 영어단어를 듣고 해당 번호를 쓰시오. 그 다음, 빈칸에 우리말을 쓰시오. 🎧73

direct ☐	probably ☐	conversation ☐	seem ☐
_____	_____	_____	_____
patient ☐	lay ☐	package ☐	pleasure ☐
_____	_____	_____	_____

Ⓑ 다음 우리말에 해당하는 영어단어를 쓰시오.

1 고래 _____   2 금지하다 _____

3 아주 작은 _____   4 임무 _____

5 영향 _____   6 잘못 _____

7 (병 등에) 시달리다 _____

436	**medicine** [médisin]	阌 의약품, 의학

- Take this **medicine** three times a day. 이 약을 하루에 세 번 복용하세요.
- My cousin went abroad to study   . 내 사촌은 의학을 공부하러 해외로 갔다.

437	**shadow** [ʃǽdou]	阌 그림자

- The dog is looking at its **shadow**. 개가 자신의 그림자를 바라보고 있다.
- The baby was afraid of his own   . 아기는 자신의 그림자를 보고 무서워했다.

438	**talent** [tǽlənt]	阌 재능

- The young girl has a **talent** for acting. 그 어린 여자아이는 연기에 대한 재능이 있다.
- We were surprised at Anna's musical   . 우리는 Anna의 음악적 재능에 놀랐다.

439	**mobile** [móubəl]	阍 이동식의, 이동할 수 있는

- It was easy to install the **mobile** air conditioner. 이동식 에어컨을 설치하는 것은 쉬웠다.
- The   library has over 5,000 books. 그 이동도서관은 5천 권이 넘는 책을 보유하고 있다.

440	**indoor** [índɔ̀ːr]	阍 실내의

- The hotel has an **indoor** swimming pool. 그 호텔에는 실내 수영장이 있다.
- I like   activities like playing video games.
  나는 비디오게임과 같은 실내 활동을 좋아한다.

441	**effort** [éfərt]	阌 노력

- I'll make every **effort** to help you. 나는 너를 돕기 위해 모든 노력을 다할 거야.
- You can't succeed without   . 노력 없이는 성공할 수 없다.

442	**liberty** [líbərti]	阌 자유 liberal 阍 자유의

- We visited the Statue of **Liberty** in New York. 우리는 뉴욕에 있는 자유의 여신상을 방문했다.
- The slaves fought for their   . 노예들은 자유를 위해 싸웠다.

443	**sweet** [swiːt]	阍 달콤한, 단

- Grapes and cherries usually taste **sweet**. 포도와 체리는 보통 단 맛이 난다.
- My family likes   apple pie. 우리 가족은 달콤한 사과 파이를 좋아한다.

444	**sentence** [séntəns]	阌 문장

- Make a **sentence** with these words. 이 단어들로 문장을 만드세요.
- Put a period at the end of the   . 문장 끝에는 마침표를 찍으세요.

445	**tip** [tip]	阌 뾰족한 끝, 조언, 봉사료

- The **tip** of the pencil is sharp. 그 연필 끝이 날카롭다.
- Here are some   s for saving money. 여기 돈을 절약할 수 있는 몇 가지 조언이 있다.

446 beard
[biərd]

명 턱수염
- The old man had a long **beard**. 그 노인은 긴 턱수염이 있었다.
- I don't want to grow a _____. 나는 턱수염을 기르고 싶지 않아.

447 disagree
[dìsəgríː]

동 의견이 다르다, 동의하지 않다
- My mom and dad sometimes **disagree**. 엄마와 아빠는 가끔 의견이 다르다.
- Do you agree or _____ with the decision? 너는 그 결정에 동의하니 아니면 그렇지 않니?

448 flow
[flou]
flow-flew-flown

동 (액체 등이) 흐르다
- The river **flows** into the Yellow Sea. 그 강은 황해로 흘러 들어간다.
- Water _____s from a higher level to a lower level.
  물은 높은 곳에서 낮은 곳으로 흐른다.

449 personality
[pə̀rsənǽləti]

명 성격
- My brother and I have very different **personalities**. 형과 나는 성격이 매우 다르다.
- The girl has a cheerful _____. 그 여자아이는 밝은 성격을 가지고 있다.

450 suggest
[səgdʒést]

동 제안하다   suggestion 명 제안
- Riley **suggested** going to see a baseball game. Riley는 야구 경기를 보러 가자고 제안했다.
- My sister _____ed cooking dinner for Mom and Dad.
  언니는 엄마와 아빠를 위해 저녁 식사를 준비하자고 제안했다.

Check Up

정답 p.125

A 다음 영어단어를 듣고 해당 번호를 쓰시오. 그 다음, 빈칸에 우리말을 쓰시오. 🎧75

medicine ☐	beard ☐	disagree ☐	effort ☐
_____	_____	_____	_____
shadow ☐	mobile ☐	sentence ☐	personality ☐
_____	_____	_____	_____

B 다음 우리말에 해당하는 영어단어를 쓰시오.

1 실내의 _____   2 재능 _____

3 제안하다 _____   4 (액체 등이) 흐르다 _____

5 달콤한 _____   6 뾰족한 끝 _____

7 자유 _____

A 다음 영어단어의 우리말을 쓰시오.

1 whale _____   2 medicine _____

3 talent _____   4 sentence _____

5 seem _____   6 indoor _____

7 tiny _____   8 suggest _____

9 flow _____   10 beard _____

11 liberty _____   12 personality _____

B 우리말과 일치하도록 알맞은 영어단어를 써넣어 문장을 완성하시오.

1 Why don't you join in the _____? 너도 대화에 참여하는 게 어때?

2 I want a _____ answer from Amy. 나는 Amy에게 직접적인 대답을 듣고 싶어.

3 Grapes and cherries usually taste _____. 포도와 체리는 보통 단 맛이 난다.

4 The medicine had no _____ on me. 그 약은 나에게 효과가 없었다.

5 The dog is looking at its _____. 개가 자신의 그림자를 바라보고 있다.

6 You can't succeed without _____. 노력 없이는 성공할 수 없다.

7 A nurse is caring for the old _____. 간호사가 나이 많은 환자를 돌보고 있다.

8 My mom and dad sometimes _____. 엄마와 아빠는 가끔 의견이 다르다.

9 A mailman left a _____ for you. 집배원이 네게 온 소포를 두고 갔어.

10 The two people are _____ a couple. 그 두 사람은 아마 부부일 거야.

C 다음 영어문장이 우리말과 일치하면 O, 그렇지 않으면 X를 쓰시오.

1 It's a pleasure to see you again. 당신을 다시 만나게 되어 기쁩니다. (   )

2 I have a fault to complete. 나는 끝내야 할 임무가 있어. (   )

3 The tip of the pencil is sharp. 그 연필 끝이 날카롭다. (   )

4 My dad laid his hands on my forehead. 아빠가 내 이마에 손을 올려 놓으셨다. (   )

5 I banned from a headache last night. 나는 어젯밤에 두통에 시달렸다. (   )

1 Riley _____ed going to see a baseball game. ➡ ....

2 The slaves fought for their _____. ➡ ....

3 The young girl has a _____ for acting. ➡ ....

4 Be _____ and wait for the result. ➡ ....

5 The girl has a cheerful _____. ➡ ....

6 Traveling always gives me great _____. ➡ ....

7 I'll make every _____ to help you. ➡ ....

8 The baby was afraid of his own _____. ➡ ....

9 Don't worry. It's not your _____. ➡ ....

10 The hotel has an _____ swimming pool. ➡ ....

11 Will you _____ the magazine on the table? ➡ ....

12 Japan often _____s damage by earthquakes. ➡ ....

13 Take this _____ three times a day. ➡ ....

14 Make a _____ with these words. ➡ ....

15 Who _____ed this movie? ➡ ....

16 Some _____s are swimming in the ocean. ➡ ....

17 The school _____ned using smartphones in class. ➡ ....

18 My family likes _____ apple pie. ➡ ....

19 We had a _____ about K-pop. ➡ ....

20 Here are some _____s for saving money. ➡ ....

21 Smoking has a bad _____ on your health. ➡ ....

22 The glass broke into _____ pieces. ➡ ....

23 The old man had a long _____. ➡ ....

24 Our _____ is to help the poor children. ➡ ....

25 The baby is _____ sleeping now. ➡ ....

26 What is in the _____? ➡ ....

27 Do you agree or _____ with the decision? ➡ ....

28 Jake _____s like a nice boy. ➡ ....

29 The _____ library has over 5,000 books. ➡ ....

30 The river_____s into the Yellow Sea. ➡ ....

A 영어단어는 우리말로, 우리말은 영어단어로 바꿔 쓰시오.

1 fold		26 (숫자의 합을) 세다	
2 costume		27 던지다	
3 opinion		28 결과	
4 noise		29 법	
5 pack		30 발가락	
6 spot		31 끔찍한	
7 shake		32 완벽한	
8 simple		33 10억	
9 expert		34 작가	
10 average		35 승리	
11 shout		36 평평한	
12 environment		37 설명하다	
13 path		38 아주 작은	
14 upset		39 어깨	
15 swallow		40 달콤한	
16 main		41 턱수염	
17 serious		42 엄지손가락	
18 fault		43 균형	
19 shape		44 상징	
20 shadow		45 신뢰하다	
21 recipe		46 규칙	
22 level		47 실수	
23 village		48 요금	
24 imagine		49 이로운 점	
25 skip		50 눈물	

B 우리말과 일치하도록 알맞은 영어단어를 써넣어 문장을 완성하시오.

1 I'll watch the movie and write a _____. 나는 그 영화를 보고 리뷰를 쓸 거야.

2 We used to go fishing in the _____. 우리는 개울에서 낚시를 하곤 했다.

3 The baby was in a thick _____. 그 아기는 두꺼운 담요를 덮고 있었다.

4 Hand in the _____ by next Monday. 보고서를 다음주 월요일까지 제출하세요.

5 I need a special _____ to open the lock. 그 자물쇠를 열기 위해서 특별한 도구가 필요하다.

6 Peaches are _____ in the winter. 복숭아는 겨울에 비싸다.

7 Your _____ will be delivered next week. 네 소포는 다음주에 배달될 거야.

8 Mia refused my _____ of help. Mia는 도와 주겠다는 나의 제안을 거절했다.

9 The robber was _____ed by the police officers. 그 도둑은 경찰관에 의해 체포되었다.

10 This bed is very _____. 이 침대는 매우 편안하다.

11 You can take this _____ to the airport. 이 고속도로를 타면 공항에 갈 수 있다.

12 A Korean _____ won the gold medal. 한국인 운동선수가 금메달을 땄다.

13 There is a _____ toilet in the park. 그 공원에는 공중 화장실이 있다.

14 Tie this _____ to the tree. 이 밧줄을 나무에 매시오.

15 Everyone seems to be _____. 모든 사람들이 긴장한 것 같다.

16 _____, Jason started laughing out loud. 갑자기 Jason이 크게 웃기 시작했다.

17 Is this shirt _____ in any other colors? 이 셔츠는 다른 색깔로도 구할 수 있나요?

18 I used the box as a _____. 나는 그 상자를 좌석으로 사용했다.

19 Do you want to _____ your studies? 너는 공부를 계속하고 싶니?

20 Can I borrow your _____? 망치를 빌려줄래요?

21 _____ it was dark outside, we went for a walk. 밖이 어두웠지만 우리는 산책하러 나갔다.

22 English is the _____ language. 영어는 국제적인 언어이다.

23 Mr. Green has _____ business skills. Green 씨는 사업 수완이 뛰어나다.

24 Everybody _____ Jenny will join the trip. Jenny를 제외하고 모두가 여행을 갈 것이다.

25 I'm _____ing for my cellphone. 나는 내 휴대전화를 찾고 있다.

C 다음 문장에 들어갈 알맞은 단어를 고르시오.

1 Which do you [mark / protect / prefer], coffee or tea?

2 Visitors are walking [within / toward / except] the lobby.

3 A rich man [threw / noticed / donated] 10 million dollars.

4 A cat is [wondering / separating / chasing] after a mouse.

5 What's the [purpose / mayor / speech] of your visit?

6 Lauren's hairstyle is [excellent / similar / serious] to mine.

7 The restaurant [reports / peels / serves] traditional Korean food.

8 It is [rude / equal / royal] to keep others waiting.

9 I'll make every [talent / effort / fault] to help you.

10 Spitting on the ground is [banned / melted / informed] in Singapore.

11 How many [votes / dives / warns] did the new class president get?

12 [Knock / Pack / Decorate] on the door before you come in.

13 There are two [local / narrow / tired] newspapers in our city.

14 Van Gogh painted mostly [perfect / ordinary / anxious] people.

15 The [temperature / order / pace] of the desert is very high.

16 The hotel has a/an [past / indoor / nervous] swimming pool.

17 A [dictionary / tip / sentence] shows the meaning of a word.

18 The river [bothers / flows / destroys] into the Yellow Sea.

19 Smoking has a bad [mission / effect / throat] on your health.

20 Some customers [barked / complained / spent] about their food.

21 The stage became completely dark and [typical / polite / silent].

22 There is a [palm / pile / patient] of papers on the desk.

23 Many people will [ride / attend / stick] the festival.

24 Most wool is [stuck / produced / counted] in Australia.

25 My next door neighbor made [available / outdoor / loud] noises yesterday.

D 다음 단어의 바뀐 품사를 보기 에서 찾아 빈칸에 쓰고, 그 단어의 우리말을 쓰시오.

보기
anxiety	decide	creative	protection	sudden
delivery	apology	response	please	patience
decoration	painful	description	particularly	information

1 형 patient → 명 _____ → ....

2 동 apologize → 명 _____ → ....

3 동 deliver → 명 _____ → ....

4 동 decorate → 명 _____ → ....

5 명 pleasure → 동 _____ → ....

6 형 anxious → 명 _____ → ....

7 명 decision → 동 _____ → ....

8 부 suddenly → 형 _____ → ....

9 동 respond → 명 _____ → ....

10 동 describe → 명 _____ → ....

11 동 create → 형 _____ → ....

12 형 particular → 부 _____ → ....

13 동 inform → 명 _____ → ....

14 명 pain → 형 _____ → ....

15 동 protect → 명 _____ → ....

➕ TIP

미국인들은 Halloween Day(10월 31일)에 죽은 영혼이 다시 살아나고 귀신이나 마녀가 돌아다닌다고 믿습니다. 아이들은 유령이나 괴물 등으로 분장해서 여러 집을 돌아다니며 '과자를 주지 않으면 장난을 칠 것이다!'라고 말합니다.
핼러윈과 관련된 단어와 표현에 대해 알아보도록 합시다.

☆ **costume** ── 의상, 복장 ☆ **ghost** ── 유령 ☆ **skeleton** ── 해골, 골격

☆ **Trick or treat!** ── 과자를 주지 않으면 장난을 칠 거예요! ☆ **jack-o'-lantern** ── 잭-오-랜턴 (귀신 얼굴을 새긴 호박)

Answers

⬇ 무료 다운로드 | www.ihappyhouse.co.kr

Lesson 1 Check Up ⸻ p.9

A
- pole — ⑴ 막대, 극
- physical — ⑶ 신체적인
- among — ⑷ 중에, 사이에
- serious — ⑵ 심각한, 진지한
- shoulder — ⑻ 어깨
- fortunately — ⑸ 다행히도, 운이 좋게도
- trouble — ⑹ 문제, 골칫거리
- parade — ⑺ 행진, 퍼레이드

B
1 snake
2 wise
3 tongue
4 shake
5 shape
6 beg
7 accept

Lesson 2 Check Up ⸻ p.11

A
- swallow — ⑺ 삼키다
- polite — ⑵ 예의 바른, 공손한
- environment — ⑴ 환경
- without — ⑸ ~ 없이
- pair — ⑹ 똑같은 종류의 두 물건, 쌍
- mistake — ⑷ 실수
- behavior — ⑻ 행동, 행위
- item — ⑶ 품목, 것

B
1 asleep
2 gentle
3 upset
4 midnight
5 active
6 order
7 main

Review ⸻ pp.12~13

A
1 막대, 극
2 밤 12시, 한밤중
3 어깨
4 혀
5 활동적인
6 다행히도, 운이 좋게도
7 현명한, 지혜로운
8 심각한, 진지한
9 가장 중요한, 주된
10 뱀
11 간곡히 요청하다, 빌다, 구걸하다
12 행동, 행위

B
1 among
2 order
3 accept
4 asleep
5 Swallow
6 shape
7 item
8 parade
9 polite
10 physical

C 1 O 2 X 3 O 4 O 5 X

D
1 shoulder 어깨
2 accept 받아들이다, 승인하다
3 beg 간곡히 요청하다, 빌다, 구걸하다
4 parade 행진, 퍼레이드
5 pole 막대, 극
6 asleep 잠을 자고 있는
7 without ~ 없이
8 upset 기분이 상한
9 mistake 실수
10 snake 뱀
11 active 활동적인, 적극적인
12 behavior 행동, 행위
13 main 가장 중요한, 주된
14 environment 환경
15 shape 모양, 형태
16 tongue 혀
17 physical 신체적인
18 pair 똑같은 종류의 두 물건, 쌍
19 polite 예의 바른, 공손한
20 trouble 문제, 골칫거리
21 midnight 밤 12시, 한밤중
22 order 순서, 명령, 주문, 명령하다, 주문하다
23 wise 현명한, 지혜로운
24 serious 심각한, 진지한
25 gentle 온화한, 잔잔한
26 item 품목, 것
27 swallow 삼키다
28 Fortunately 다행히도, 운이 좋게도
29 Shake 흔들리다, 흔들다
30 among 중에, 사이에

Lesson 3 Check Up ⸻ p.15

A
- position — ⑵ 위치, 자리, 자세
- goods — ⑶ 상품
- manner — ⑸ 방식, 방법, 태도
- able — ⑷ 능력이 있는, 할 수 있는
- announce — ⑹ 발표하다, 알리다
- total — ⑻ 전체의, 총합, 합계
- experience — ⑺ 경험하다, 겪다, 경험
- envelope — ⑴ 봉투

B
1 shout
2 noise
3 plus
4 simple
5 thief
6 shade
7 mud

A
- president 　 2 회장, 대통령
- billion 　 1 10억
- attention 　 4 주의, 집중, 관심
- pan 　 3 팬, 프라이팬
- orchestra 　 5 관현악단, 오케스트라
- possible 　 7 가능한
- explain 　 6 설명하다
- treasure 　 8 보물, 보물 같은 존재

B
1 alive 　　 2 limit
3 nest 　　 4 mark
5 prefer 　　 6 grab
7 trust

A
1 10억 　　 2 새 둥지, 보금자리
3 발표하다, 알리다 　　 4 상품
5 관현악단, 오케스트라 　　 6 경험하다, 겪다, 경험
7 꽉 붙잡다, 쥐다 　　 8 위치, 자리, 자세
9 회장, 대통령 　　 10 신뢰하다, 믿다, 신뢰, 믿음
11 가능한 　　 12 보물, 보물 같은 존재

B
1 limit 　　 2 shade
3 envelope 　　 4 simple
5 shout 　　 6 manner
7 total 　　 8 thief
9 mud 　　 10 plus

C 1 O 　 2 O 　 3 X 　 4 O 　 5 X

D
1 president 회장, 대통령
2 envelope 봉투
3 nest 새 둥지, 보금자리
4 noise 소음
5 able 능력이 있는, 할 수 있는
6 orchestra 관현악단, 오케스트라
7 explain 설명하다
8 mud 진흙
9 shout 소리를 지르다, 외치다
10 possible 가능한
11 thief 도둑
12 mark 표시하다, 자국, 흔적
13 simple 간단한, 단순한
14 alive 살아 있는
15 grab 꽉 붙잡다, 쥐다

16 goods 상품
17 manner 방식, 방법, 태도
18 shade 그늘
19 position 위치, 자리, 자세
20 prefer 더 좋아하다, 선호하다
21 total 전체의, 총합, 합계
22 attention 주의, 집중, 관심
23 Plus 더하기, 게다가
24 billion 10억
25 announce 발표하다, 알리다
26 pan 팬, 프라이팬
27 limit 제한하다, 제한
28 trust 신뢰하다, 믿다, 신뢰, 믿음
29 treasure 보물, 보물 같은 존재
30 experience 경험하다, 겪다, 경험

A
- post 　 1 게시하다, 부치다
- favor 　 3 부탁, 도움, 호의
- master 　 2 주인, 달인, 대가, 완전히 익히다, 통달하다
- avoid 　 4 ~가 발생하는 것을 막다, 사람을 피하다
- although 　 5 비록 ~이지만
- typical 　 7 전형적인, 보통의
- handle 　 6 손잡이, 손으로 만지다, 다루다, 처리하다
- blossom 　 8 꽃, 꽃이 피다

B
1 strange 　　 2 maybe
3 unique 　　 4 cancel
5 share 　　 6 award
7 blow

A
- balance 　 5 균형, 균형을 잡다
- matter 　 4 문제, 일, 문제가 되다, 중요하다
- praise 　 3 칭찬하다, 칭찬, 찬사
- occur 　 1 발생하다, 일어나다
- border 　 6 국경, 경계
- tough 　 7 매우 어려운, 질긴, 거친
- provide 　 8 제공하다, 주다
- argue 　 2 말로 다투다, 주장하다

B
1 few 　　 2 shine
3 count 　　 4 relax
5 reason 　　 6 harm
7 price

Review — pp.24~25

A
1 제공하다, 주다 | 2 국경, 경계
3 이상한 | 4 취소하다
5 거의 없는 | 6 칭찬하다, 칭찬, 찬사
7 게시하다, 부치다 | 8 바람이 불다, 입으로 불다
9 문제, 일, 문제가 되다, 중요하다 | 10 세다
11 ~가 발생하는 것을 막다, 사람을 피하다
12 균형, 균형을 잡다

B
1 price | 2 reason
3 handle | 4 argue
5 favor | 6 harm
7 award | 8 Maybe
9 share | 10 Typical

C
1 X 2 O 3 O 4 X 5 X

D
1 reason 이유
2 border 국경, 경계
3 praise 칭찬하다, 칭찬, 찬사
4 avoid ~가 발생하는 것을 막다, 사람을 피하다
5 shine 빛나다, 광을 내다
6 matter 문제, 일, 문제가 되다, 중요하다
7 blow 바람이 불다, 입으로 불다
8 few 거의 없는
9 Maybe 아마, 어쩌면
10 tough 매우 어려운, 질긴, 거친
11 balance 균형, 균형을 잡다
12 Although 비록 ~이지만
13 award 상, 주다, 수여하다
14 strange 이상한
15 harm 피해, 해를 끼치다
16 typical 전형적인, 보통의
17 occur 발생하다, 일어나다
18 favor 부탁, 도움, 호의
19 cancel 취소하다
20 post 게시하다, 부치다
21 relax 쉬다, 진정하다
22 handle 손잡이, 손으로 만지다, 다루다, 처리하다
23 argue 말로 다투다, 주장하다
24 count 세다
25 price 가격
26 blossom 꽃, 꽃이 피다
27 share 공유하다
28 master 주인, 달인, 대가, 완전히 익히다, 통달하다
29 unique 독특한, 유일한, 하나뿐인
30 provide 제공하다, 주다

Lesson 7 Check Up — p.27

A
• usual — ④ 평상시의, 보통의
• outdoor — ① 야외의
• volume — ⑧ 소리 크기, 볼륨
• reply — ⑦ 대답, 대답하다, 답장하다
• flash — ② 번쩍임, 번쩍이다
• purpose — ③ 목적
• bother — ⑤ 신경을 쓰다, 귀찮게 하다
• pollution — ⑥ 오염

B
1 pond | 2 mayor
3 horror | 4 prepare
5 arrow | 6 bark
7 spend

Lesson 8 Check Up — p.29

A
• bullet — ⑥ 총알
• degree — ③ 도, 학위
• volunteer — ⑤ 자원봉사자, 자발적으로 하다, 자원봉사하다
• quality — ④ 품질, 자질, 품질이 우수한
• mechanic — ⑦ 정비사
• privacy — ② 사생활
• vehicle — ① 차량, 탈것
• rhythm — ⑧ 리듬

B
1 ignore | 2 stick
3 silent | 4 flat
5 own | 6 attack
7 beat

Review — pp.30~31

A
1 화살, 화살표 | 2 쓰다, 소비하다
3 오염 | 4 조용한, 고요한
5 준비하다, 마련하다 | 6 정비사
7 평평한, 잔잔한 | 8 신경을 쓰다, 귀찮게 하다
9 짖다 | 10 무시하다, 모르는 체하다
11 자원봉사자, 자발적으로 하다, 자원봉사하다
12 연못

B
1 outdoor | 2 degree
3 horror | 4 vehicle
5 mayor | 6 purpose
7 attack | 8 usual
9 own | 10 flash

C 1 O 2 X 3 O 4 O 5 X

D 1 flat 평평한, 잔잔한
2 attack 공격하다, 공격
3 volume 소리 크기, 볼륨
4 stick 막대기, 찌르다, 붙이다
5 horror 공포
6 degree 도, 학위
7 purpose 목적
8 outdoor 외부의
9 own 소유하다, 자기 자신의
10 pond 연못
11 bother 신경을 쓰다, 귀찮게 하다
12 usual 평상시의, 보통의
13 spent 쓰다, 소비하다
14 mechanic 정비사
15 rhythm 리듬
16 volunteer 자원봉사자, 자발적으로 하다, 자원봉사하다
17 mayor 시장
18 bark 짖다
19 bullet 총알
20 flash 번쩍임, 번쩍이다
21 ignore 무시하다, 모르는 체하다
22 prepare 준비하다, 마련하다
23 quality 품질, 자질, 품질이 좋은
24 vehicle 차량, 탈것
25 reply 대답, 대답하다, 답장하다
26 silent 조용한, 고요한
27 pollution 오염
28 privacy 사생활
29 arrow 화살
30 beat 이기다, 때리다, 두드리다, 박자

Lesson 9 Check Up ·········· p.33

A • slide   ⑦ 미끄러지다, 미끄럼틀
• bin   ① 통, 쓰레기통
• blank   ⑧ 빈, 비어 있는, 빈칸
• rather   ③ 상당히, 꽤
• bully   ② 약자를 괴롭히다, 따돌리다,
         약자를 괴롭히는 사람
• imagine   ⑥ 상상하다
• warn   ④ 위험을 알리다, 미리 주의를 주다, 경고하다
• float   ⑤ 떠다니다, 물에 뜨다

B 1 still   2 drawer
3 rule   4 vote

5 melt   6 process
7 role

Lesson 10 Check Up ·········· p.35

A • realize   ⑤ 깨닫다, 알아차리다
• weigh   ⑥ 무게가 ~이다, 무게를 재다
• pretend   ④ ~인 척하다
• forecast   ② 예측, 예보, 예측하다
• society   ③ 사회
• blind   ⑧ 눈이 보이지 않는, 시각 장애의, 블라인드
• past   ⑦ 지나간, 이전의, 과거
• a bit   ① 조금, 약간

B 1 ease   2 plate
3 mental   4 produce
5 include   6 storm
7 whole

Review ·········· pp.36~37

A 1 지나간, 이전의, 과거   2 사회
3 빈, 비어 있는, 빈칸   4 상상하다
5 깨닫다, 알아차리다   6 ~인 척하다
7 폭풍   8 전체의
9 조금, 약간   10 녹다
11 눈이 보이지 않는, 시각 장애의, 블라인드
12 서랍

B 1 still   2 mental
3 plate   4 process
5 vote   6 role
7 rather   8 rule
9 float   10 weigh

C 1 O 2 O 3 X 4 O 5 O

D 1 bin 통, 쓰레기통
2 role 역할, 배역
3 imagine 상상하다
4 warn 위험을 알리다, 미리 주의를 주다, 경고하다
5 blank 빈, 비어 있는, 빈칸
6 ease 쉬움, 편안함
7 rather 상당히, 꽤
8 mental 정신적인
9 realize 깨닫다, 알아차리다
10 drawer 서랍

11 past 지나간, 이전의, 과거
12 float 떠다니다, 물에 뜨다
13 produce 생산하다, 만들다
14 storm 폭풍
15 rule 규칙
16 a bit 조금, 약간
17 weigh 무게가 ~이다, 무게를 재다
18 vote 투표하다, 표, 투표
19 melt 녹다
20 plate 접시
21 process 과정, 절차, 처리하다
22 bully 약자를 괴롭히다, 따돌리다, 약자를 괴롭히는 사람
23 slide 미끄러지다, 미끄럼틀
24 blind 눈이 보이지 않는, 시각 장애의, 블라인드
25 society 사회
26 pretend ~인 척하다
27 include 포함하다, 포함시키다
28 whole 전체의
29 forecast 예측, 예보, 예측하다
30 still 여전히, 아직도

누적 테스트 150 ·········· pp.38~41

A 1 중에, 사이에
2 문제, 골칫거리
3 신체적인
4 더하기, 게다가
5 경험하다, 겪다, 경험
6 그늘
7 도둑
8 상품
9 똑같은 종류의 두 물건, 쌍
10 10억
11 상, 주다, 수여하다
12 꽃, 꽃이 피다
13 말로 다투다, 주장하다
14 균형, 균형을 잡다
15 정신적인
16 사회
17 거의 없는
18 국경, 경계
19 대답, 대답하다, 답장하다
20 보물, 보물 같은 존재
21 꽉 붙잡다, 쥐다
22 봉투
23 간곡히 요청하다, 빌다, 구걸하다

26 although
27 snake
28 parade
29 midnight
30 nest
31 environment
32 main
33 master
34 unique
35 handle
36 count
37 occur
38 pond
39 spend
40 own
41 vehicle
42 rule
43 blank
44 strange
45 blow
46 position
47 behavior
48 warn

24 막대, 극
25 어깨

B 1 mark
3 matter
5 active
7 simple
9 post
11 prepare
13 Stick
15 shape
17 mistake
19 flat
21 ignore
23 quality
25 without

2 avoid
4 rather
6 swallow
8 shout
10 cancel
12 purpose
14 manner
16 accept
18 share
20 praise
22 relax
24 whole

C 1 serious
3 shouting
5 president
7 vote
9 blind
11 mud
13 still
15 alive
17 melts
19 produces
21 upset
23 typical
25 bother

2 price
4 possible
6 purpose
8 plates
10 order
12 prefer
14 tongue
16 orchestra
18 polite
20 include
22 favor
24 harm

49 shake
50 wise

D 1 seriously 심각하게
2 fortunate 다행인
3 noisy 시끄러운
4 ability 능력
5 announcement 발표
6 pollute 오염시키다
7 shiny 빛나는
8 horrible 무서운, 끔찍한
9 usually 보통
10 private 사적인
11 silence 고요함, 정적
12 imagination 상상
13 easy 쉬운
14 production 생산
15 weight 무게

Lesson 11   Check Up ·········· p.43

A
- blanket — ⑥ 담요, 이불
- sore — ③ 아픈, 따가운
- grade — ⑧ 등급, 점수, 학년
- breathe — ⑦ 숨쉬다, 호흡하다
- recognize — ④ 알아보다, 인식하다
- increase — ① 증가하다, 증가
- punish — ⑤ 벌을 주다
- forgive — ② 용서하다

B
1 hole   2 sense
3 wheel   4 humid
5 pattern   6 capital
7 million

Lesson 12   Check Up ·········· p.45

A
- intelligent — ⑥ 지능이 높은, 똑똑한
- miracle — ⑤ 기적
- spoil — ③ 망치다, 못쓰게 만들다
- stretch — ① 늘이다, 뻗다
- underground — ② 지하의, 지하에
- pepper — ⑦ 후추
- fortune — ⑧ 재산, 운
- sheet — ④ 침대에 까는 천, 시트, 종이 한 장

B
1 pure   2 fair
3 wonder   4 cave
5 regular   6 bride
7 chase

Review ·········· pp.46~47

A
1 백만   2 망치다, 못쓰게 만들다
3 기적   4 아픈, 따가운
5 알아보다, 인식하다   6 쫓다, 추격하다
7 지능이 높은, 똑똑한   8 증가하다, 증가
9 감각, 감지하다, 느끼다   10 궁금해하다
11 다른 것이 섞이지 않은, 순수한   12 재산, 운

B
1 cave   2 pepper
3 hole   4 capital
5 bride   6 humid
7 breathe   8 fair
9 grade   10 regular

C 1 ○   2 X   3 ○   4 ○   5 X

D
1 million 백만
2 cave 동굴
3 grade 등급, 점수, 학년
4 recognize 알아보다, 인식하다
5 increase 증가하다, 증가
6 punish 벌을 주다
7 stretch 늘이다, 뻗다
8 wheel 바퀴, 핸들
9 fair 공정한, 박람회
10 sore 아픈, 따가운
11 sheet 침대에 까는 천, 시트, 종이 한 장
12 pepper 후추
13 humid 습한
14 capital 수도, 대문자의
15 blanket 담요, 이불
16 pattern 무늬, 패턴, 양식
17 regular 정기적인, 규칙적인, 횟수가 잦은
18 fortune 재산, 운
19 spoil 망치다, 못쓰게 만들다
20 forgive 용서하다
21 miracle 기적
22 bride 신부
23 pure 다른 것이 섞이지 않은, 순수한
24 sense 감각, 감지하다, 느끼다
25 wonder 궁금해하다
26 intelligent 지능이 높은, 똑똑한
27 chase 쫓다, 추격하다
28 underground 지하의, 지하에
29 breathe 숨쉬다, 호흡하다
30 hole 구멍

Lesson 13   Check Up ·········· p.49

A
- piece — ① 조각
- shower — ⑤ 샤워, 소나기
- such — ③ 그러한, 그런, 너무나
- yell — ④ 소리를 지르다, 고함치다
- raise — ② 들어올리다, 기르다
- spirit — ⑧ 정신, 영혼
- celebrate — ⑦ 축하하다, 기념하다
- spread — ⑥ 펼치다, 퍼지다, 확산되다

B
1 final   2 monster
3 remain   4 survey
5 cheek   6 invent
7 chest

Lesson 14 Check Up p.51

A
- challenge — ⑤ 도전하다, 하기 어려운 일
- purse — ④ 지갑, 작은 여성용 가방
- vacation — ⑧ 휴가, 방학
- abroad — ⑥ 해외에서, 해외로
- flood — ③ 홍수, 물이 넘치게 하다
- muscle — ② 근육
- stairs — ① 계단
- reach — ⑦ ~에 이르다, 도달하다, 닿다

B
1 local   2 chin
3 repair   4 silver
5 fur   6 greet
7 sweat

Review .... pp.52~53

A
1 괴물   2 가슴, 흉부, 상자
3 계단   4 소리를 지르다, 고함치다
5 은   6 조각
7 턱   8 휴가, 방학
9 발명하다   10 도전하다, 하기 어려운 일
11 마지막, 최종의   12 홍수, 물이 넘치게 하다

B
1 muscle   2 greet
3 celebrate   4 local
5 fur   6 cheek
7 purse   8 reach
9 shower   10 such

C 1 O   2 O   3 X   4 X   5 O

D
1 piece 조각
2 vacation 휴가, 방학
3 greet 인사하다
4 such 그러한, 그런, 너무나
5 remain 여전히 ~이다, 남아 있다
6 silver 은
7 fur 털, 모피
8 challenge 도전하다, 하기 어려운 일
9 survey 설문 조사, 설문 조사하다
10 final 마지막, 최종의
11 muscle 근육
12 flood 홍수, 물이 넘치게 하다
13 sweat 땀을 흘리다, 땀
14 chest 가슴, 흉부, 상자
15 cheek 볼, 뺨

16 chin 턱
17 repair 수리하다, 고치다
18 shower 샤워, 소나기
19 reach ~에 이르다, 도달하다, 닿다
20 local 그 지역의, 근처의
21 invent 발명하다
22 celebrate 축하하다, 기념하다
23 abroad 해외에서, 해외로
24 raise 들어올리다, 기르다
25 purse 지갑, 작은 여성용 가방
26 spread 펼치다, 퍼지다, 확산되다
27 stairs 계단
28 monster 괴물
29 yell 소리를 지르다, 고함치다
30 spirit 정신, 영혼

Lesson 15 Check Up p.55

A
- screen — ② 화면
- since — ⑤ ~부터, ~한 때로부터, ~ 때문에
- research — ④ 연구, 조사, 연구하다, 조사하다
- achieve — ⑥ 이루다, 달성하다
- university — ⑦ 대학
- nearby — ③ 가까이의, 근처의
- choir — ⑧ 합창단, 성가대
- hall — ① 복도, 홀, 넓은 방

B
1 statue   2 pine
3 wing   4 seed
5 narrow   6 loss
7 chop

Lesson 16 Check Up p.57

A
- advertise — ① 광고하다, 광고를 내다
- straight — ⑧ 똑바로, 곧장, 똑바른, 곧은
- disappear — ⑤ 보이지 않게 되다, 사라지다
- comfortable — ⑥ 편안한, 안락한
- terrible — ⑦ 끔찍한
- medium — ④ 중간의
- dive — ② 물속으로 뛰어들다, 잠수하다
- receive — ③ 받다

B
1 slim   2 guest
3 neat   4 clap
5 respect   6 heel
7 cure

118

Review · pp.58~59

A
1 날개
2 물속으로 뛰어들다, 잠수하다
3 박수를 치다
4 썰다, 자르다
5 끔찍한
6 받다
7 좁은
8 손실, 상실
9 소나무, 솔
10 조각상
11 가까이의, 근처의
12 중간의

B
1 screen
2 neat
3 slim
4 comfortable
5 achieve
6 seed
7 heel
8 advertise
9 respect
10 since

C 1 O   2 X   3 X   4 O   5 O

D
1 wing 날개
2 nearby 가까이의, 근처의
3 seed 씨, 씨앗
4 slim 날씬한, 얇은
5 cure 치료하다, 치유하다, 치료
6 guest 손님, 게스트
7 respect 존경, 존중, 존경하다, 존중하다
8 since ~부터, ~한 때로부터, ~ 때문에
9 clap 박수를 치다
10 terrible 끔찍한
11 choir 합창단, 성가대
12 straight 똑바로, 곧장, 똑바른, 곧은
13 dive 물에 뛰어들다, 잠수하다
14 university 대학
15 advertise 광고하다, 광고를 내다
16 screen 화면
17 loss 손실, 상실
18 narrow 좁은
19 medium 중간의
20 comfortable 편안한, 안락한
21 statue 조각상
22 heel 발뒤꿈치, 굽
23 disappear 보이지 않게 되다, 사라지다
24 hall 복도, 홀, 넓은 방
25 research 연구, 조사, 연구하다, 조사하다
26 achieve 이루다, 달성하다
27 neat 단정한, 정돈된
28 chop 썰다, 자르다
29 receive 받다
30 pine 소나무, 솔

Lesson 17 Check Up · p.61

A
- disappoint · ⑤ 실망시키다
- recommend · ⑥ 추천하다
- hesitate · ④ 망설이다, 머뭇거리다
- height · ③ 높이, 키
- through · ⑧ ~을 통해, 관통하여
- community · ② 지역 공동체, 모임
- pop · ① 터지다, 터트리다
- necessary · ⑦ 필요한

B
1 aisle
2 metal
3 row
4 strike
5 dot
6 soil
7 complain

Lesson 18 Check Up · p.63

A
- discount · ④ 할인, 할인하다
- structure · ⑦ 구조, 구조물, 건축물
- reduce · ② 줄이다, 감소시키다
- nervous · ⑤ 긴장한, 두려워하는
- complete · ① 완성하다, 끝내다, 완전한, 부족함이 없는
- compare · ⑧ 비교하다
- household · ③ 가정
- modern · ⑥ 현대의, 현대적인

B
1 enemy
2 allow
3 rumor
4 soldier
5 poster
6 tie
7 excuse

Review · pp.64~65

A
1 점
2 적
3 군인
4 소문, 루머
5 현대의, 현대적인
6 가정
7 불평하다, 항의하다
8 높이, 키
9 비교하다
10 긴장한, 두려워하는
11 통로
12 망설이다, 머뭇거리다

B
1 reduce
2 structure
3 metal
4 excuse
5 disappoint
6 discount
7 tie
8 struck
9 row
10 soil

C 1 X 2 O 3 O 4 O 5 X

D 1 soil 흙, 토양

2 recommend 추천하다

3 height 높이, 키

4 community 지역 공동체, 모임

5 struck 치다, 부딪치다

6 discount 할인, 할인하다

7 pop 터지다, 터트리다

8 disappoint 실망시키다

9 poster 벽보, 포스터

10 dot 점

11 modern 현대의, 현대적인

12 aisle 통로

13 through ~을 통해, 관통하여

14 complain 불평하다, 항의하다

15 household 가정

16 allow 허락하다, 허가하다

17 rumor 소문, 루머

18 hesitate 망설이다, 머뭇거리다

19 tie 매다, 묶다, 넥타이

20 metal 금속

21 excuse 용서하다, 이유, 변명

22 nervous 긴장한, 두려워하는

23 row 줄, 열

24 necessary 필요한

25 complete 완성하다, 끝내다, 완전한, 부족함이 없는

26 structure 구조, 구조물, 건축물

27 enemy 적

28 compare 비교하다

29 reduce 줄이다, 감소시키다

30 solider 군인

Lesson 19 Check Up ···················· p.67

A • sunshine 　[1] 햇빛

• separate 　[5] 따로 떨어진, 분리하다

• confuse 　[7] 헷갈리게 하다, 혼동하다

• relieve 　[6] 줄이다, 완화시키다

• confident 　[3] 자신감 있는, 확신하는

• ill 　[4] 아픈, 병에 걸린

• native 　[2] 태어난 곳의, ~ 태생/출신인 사람

• speech 　[8] 연설, 강연

B 1 equal 　　　　　2 edge

3 amazing 　　　　4 nod

5 square 　　　　　6 hug

7 tired

Lesson 20 Check Up ···················· p.69

A • education 　[7] 교육

• officer 　[1] 장교, 공무원, 관리

• surface 　[6] 표면

• respond 　[2] 응답하다, 반응하다

• amount 　[8] 양

• improve 　[3] 나아지다, 향상시키다

• contact 　[5] 접촉, 연락, 접촉하다, 연락하다

• continent 　[4] 대륙

B 1 stamp 　　　　　2 sight

3 title 　　　　　　4 instead

5 normal 　　　　　6 protect

7 flight

Review ··· pp.70~71

A 1 응답하다, 반응하다 　　2 대신에

3 보호하다 　　　　　　4 표면

5 비행, 비행기 　　　　　6 끄덕이다

7 대륙 　　　　　　　　8 가장자리, 모서리, 날

9 지친, 피곤한 　　　　　10 양

11 교육 　　　　　　　　12 우표, 도장

B 1 Separate 　　　　　2 sunshine

3 equal 　　　　　　4 title

5 confuse 　　　　　6 native

7 square 　　　　　8 contact

9 Normal 　　　　　10 speech

C 1 O 2 O 3 O 4 X 5 O

D 1 sight 시력, 광경

2 surface 표면

3 stamp 우표, 도장

4 speech 연설, 강연

5 separate 따로 떨어진

6 tired 피곤한, 지친

7 ill 아픈, 병에 걸린

8 flight 비행, 비행기

9 native 태어난 곳의, 태생/출신인 사람

10 normal 보통의, 일반적인

11 instead 대신에

12 contact 접촉, 연락, 접촉하다, 연락하다

13 relieve 줄이다, 완화시키다

14 protect 보호하다

15 amount 양

16 confident 자신감 있는, 확신하는
17 edge 가장자리, 모서리, 날
18 confuse 헷갈리게 하다, 혼동하다
19 continent 대륙
20 nod 끄덕이다
21 officer 장교, 공무원, 관리
22 hug 끌어안다, 포옹하다, 포옹
23 improve 나아지다, 향상시키다
24 amazing 놀라운, 굉장한
25 equal 같은, 동등한, 평등한
26 respond 응답하다, 반응하다
27 sunshine 햇빛
28 square 정사각형, 정사각형의
29 title 제목
30 education 교육

7 cure
9 vacation
11 terrible
13 tie
15 million
17 breathe
19 challenge
21 contact
23 spread
25 rumor

8 sense
10 remain
12 straight
14 medium
16 Shower
18 sweat
20 local
22 piece
24 respect

누적 테스트 300 .... pp. 72~75

A
1 용서하다
2 방식, 방법, 태도
3 수리하다, 고치다
4 발표하다, 알리다
5 가능한
6 기적
7 궁금해하다
8 표면
9 지하의, 지하에
10 근육
11 대답, 대답하다, 답장하다
12 행동, 행위
13 소리를 지르다, 고함치다
14 늘이다, 뻗다
15 순서, 명령, 주문, 명령하다, 주문하다   40 stairs
16 해외에서, 해외로
17 양
18 신체적인
19 대학
20 이루다, 달성하다
21 가까이의, 근처의
22 받다
23 가장 중요한, 주된
24 불평하다, 항의하다
25 추천하다

26 limit
27 punish
28 melt
29 fair
30 celebrate
31 society
32 prepare
33 sunshine
34 include
35 stamp
36 pond
37 shine
38 announce
39 silver
41 chin
42 humid
43 greet
44 ignore
45 square
46 survey
47 clap
48 soil
49 price
50 modern

B
1 reach
3 screen
5 edge

2 hole
4 tired
6 narrow

C
1 argue
3 hall
5 nodded
7 explained
9 statue
11 flood
13 improve
15 nervous
17 continents
19 punished
21 disappeared
23 metal
25 increasing

2 melting
4 Normal
6 reduce
8 row
10 muscles
12 raised
14 compare
16 vehicle
18 sore
20 slim
22 canceled
24 wheels

D
1 necessarily 필히
2 intelligence 지능
3 separately 각각
4 finally 마지막으로, 마침내
5 breath 호흡
6 advertisement 광고
7 confidence 확신
8 high 높은
9 educate 교육시키다
10 illness 병
11 see 보다
12 comfort 편안함
13 protection 보호
14 fly 날다, 비행하다
15 celebration 축하

Lesson 21 Check Up .... p. 77

A
• opinion   ⑤ 의견
• toward   ③ ~쪽으로, ~을 향하여
• public   ⑦ 일반인들, 대중, 일반인의, 모두를 위한,
                  공공의
• switch   ① 스위치, 바꾸다, 전환하다

- continue   ⑧ 계속하다, 지속되다
- anxious   ④ 걱정하는, 간절히 원하는
- result   ② 결과, 발생하다
- notice   ⑥ 알아차리다, 안내, 예고

B 1 stream   2 emotion
3 joke   4 fold
5 throw   6 costume
7 silly

Lesson 22   Check Up ·········· p.79

A
- similar   ⑤ 비슷한, 유사한
- hammer   ⑥ 망치
- equipment   ① 장비
- symbol   ② 상징, 기호
- courage   ⑧ 용기
- creature   ⑦ 생물, 생명체
- trade   ③ 거래, 무역, 거래하다
- interesting   ④ 흥미로운

B 1 apologize   2 lead
3 offer   4 ordinary
5 thick   6 recipe
7 review

Review ·········· pp.80~81

A 1 던지다   2 요리법, 레시피
3 개울, 시내   4 걱정하는, 간절히 원하는
5 의상, 복장   6 흥미로운
7 일반인들, 대중, 일반인의, 모두를 위한, 공공의
8 이끌다, ~으로 이어지다, 연결되다
9 장비   10 제안하다, 제안
11 의견   12 사과하다

B 1 symbol   2 emotion
3 courage   4 result
5 joke   6 similar
7 hammer   8 thick
9 fold   10 Review

C 1 X   2 O   3 O   4 O   5 X

D 1 joke 농담, 농담하다
2 opinion 의견
3 Creature 생물, 생명체
4 recipe 요리법, 레시피

5 stream 개울, 시내
6 silly 어리석은, 바보 같은, 우스꽝스러운
7 similar 비슷한, 유사한
8 result 결과, 발생하다
9 lead 이끌다, ~로 이어지다, 연결되다
10 offer 제안, 제안하다
11 costume 의상, 복장
12 equipment 장비
13 anxious 걱정하는, 간절히 원하는
14 trade 거래, 무역, 거래하다
15 switch 스위치, 바꾸다, 전환하다
16 Throw 던지다
17 ordinary 보통의, 일상적인
18 Fold 접다
19 hammer 망치
20 symbol 상징, 기호
21 apologize 사과하다
22 continue 계속하다, 지속되다
23 thick 두꺼운
24 emotion 감정
25 toward ~쪽으로, ~을 향하여
26 courage 용기
27 review 검토하다, 복습하다, 검토, 평가, 리뷰
28 interesting 흥미로운
29 notice 알아차리다, 안내, 예고
30 public 일반인들, 대중, 일반인의, 모두를 위한, 공공의

Lesson 23   Check Up ·········· p.83

A
- excellent   ① 뛰어난, 훌륭한
- situation   ⑥ 상황
- serve   ② 제공하다, 내오다, 시중들다
- arrest   ⑧ 체포하다
- international   ⑤ 국제적인
- though   ⑦ ~이지만, 그러나, 하지만
- harvest   ③ 수확 (시기), 수확량, 거두다, 수확하다
- record   ④ 기록, 기록하다

B 1 level   2 roll
3 curl   4 task
5 trick   6 pain
7 dictionary

Lesson 24 ▶ Check Up ········· p.85

A
- decision — ⑦ 결정
- pile — ⑧ 쌓아 놓은 것, 더미
- create — ② 만들어 내다
- athlete — ① 운동선수
- palm — ⑤ 손바닥
- highway — ⑥ 고속도로
- royal — ③ 국왕의, 왕족의
- thumb — ④ 엄지손가락

B
1 tear   2 except
3 twin   4 lift
5 pace   6 skip
7 report

Review ········· pp.86~87

A
1 사전   2 수준, 단계
3 고속도로   4 체포하다
5 상황   6 국제적인
7 쌓아 놓은 것, 더미   8 손바닥
9 일, 업무   10 ~을 제외하고
11 국왕의, 왕족의   12 운동선수

B
1 record   2 decision
3 pace   4 lift
5 excellent   6 twin
7 pain   8 thumb
9 skip   10 roll

C 1 O   2 X   3 O   4 X   5 O

D
1 skip 거르다, 빼먹다
2 royal 국왕의, 왕족의
3 situation 상황
4 level 수준, 단계
5 arrest 체포하다
6 pile 쌓아 놓은 것, 더미
7 task 일, 업무
8 create 만들어 내다
9 serve 제공하다, 내오다, 시중들다
10 tear 눈물, 찢다
11 highway 고속도로
12 curl 곱슬거리게 하다, 동그랗게 말리게 하다, 곱슬곱슬한 머리카락
13 roll 구르다, 굴러가다
14 palm 손바닥
15 pace 속도

---

16 thumb 엄지손가락
17 excellent 뛰어난, 훌륭한
18 athlete 운동선수
19 lift 들어 올리다
20 though ~이지만, 그러나, 하지만
21 international 국제적인
22 record 기록, 기록하다
23 decision 결정
24 dictionary 사전
25 pain 통증, 고통
26 report 알리다, 보도하다, 보고하다, 보고(서)
27 trick 속임수, 장난, 속이다
28 twin 쌍둥이, 쌍둥이의
29 harvest 수확 (시기), 수확량, 거두다, 수확하다
30 except ~을 제외하고

Lesson 25 ▶ Check Up ········· p.89

A
- peel — ① 껍질을 벗기다, 껍질
- expensive — ⑦ 비싼
- ride — ② 직접 몰다, 타다, 타고 가다
- decorate — ⑧ 장식하다, 꾸미다
- temperature — ③ 온도
- deliver — ⑥ 배달하다
- journal — ④ 일기, 잡지
- attend — ⑤ 참석하다, 다니다

B
1 toe   2 spot
3 rude   4 clinic
5 list   6 pack
7 knight

Lesson 26 ▶ Check Up ········· p.91

A
- view — ③ 생각, 의견, 전망
- judge — ⑧ 판사, 심사위원, 판단하다
- knock — ② 두드리다, 노크하다
- benefit — ① 이로운 점
- determine — ④ 결정하다
- available — ⑦ 이용 가능한, 구할 수 있는
- delight — ⑤ 기쁨, 기쁨을 주다
- panic — ⑥ 극도의 공포, 어쩔 줄 모르게 하다

B
1 rope   2 scare
3 expert   4 loud
5 steam   6 perfect
7 tool

Review .... pp.92~93

A
1 기사
2 결정하다
3 일기, 잡지
4 싸다
5 겁을 주다, 무섭게 만들다
6 완벽한, 가장 좋은
7 전문가
8 온도
9 시끄러운, 소리가 큰
10 기쁨, 기쁨을 주다
11 진료소, 병원
12 목록, 명단

B
1 steam
2 deliver
3 rude
4 toe
5 expensive
6 Judge
7 tool
8 attend
9 rope
10 knock

C
1 X   2 X   3 O   4 O   5 X

D
1 Steam 증기, 김
2 available 이용 가능한, 구할 수 있는
3 attend 참석하다, 다니다
4 Knock 두드리다, 노크하다
5 scare 겁을 주다, 무섭게 만들다
6 peel 껍질을 벗기다, 껍질
7 tool 도구
8 decorate 장식하다, 꾸미다
9 temperature 온도
10 delight 기쁨, 기쁨을 주다
11 rude 무례한, 버릇없는
12 expensive 비싼
13 view 생각, 의견, 전망
14 journal 일기, 잡지
15 panic 극도의 공포, 어쩔 줄 모르게 하다
16 deliver 배달하다
17 determine 결정하다
18 pack 싸다
19 ride 직접 몰다, 타다, 타고 가다
20 perfect 완벽한, 가장 좋은
21 clinic 진료소, 병원
22 toe 발가락
23 benefit 이로운 점
24 rope 밧줄
25 list 목록, 명단
26 loud 시끄러운, 소리가 큰
27 judge 판사, 심사위원, 판단하다
28 knight 기사
29 spot 반점, 얼룩, 장소
30 expert 전문가

Lesson 27 Check Up p.95

A
• village — ⑧ 마을
• particular — ① 특정한
• explore — ⑦ 탐사하다, 탐험하다
• throat — ③ 목구멍, 목
• kingdom — ⑥ 왕국
• describe — ⑤ 자세히 말하다, 묘사하다
• stomach — ② 위, 복부, 배
• photograph — ④ 사진

B
1 law
2 craft
3 author
4 search
5 average
6 victory
7 magazine

Lesson 28 Check Up p.97

A
• destroy — ⑤ 파괴하다
• match — ④ 어울리다, 성냥
• donate — ② 기부하다, 기증하다
• inform — ③ 알리다
• path — ⑧ 길
• language — ① 언어
• within — ⑥ ~ 안에, ~ 이내에
• aware — ⑦ ~을 알고 있는

B
1 fare
2 seat
3 weak
4 secret
5 pity
6 lock
7 suddenly

Review .... pp.98~99

A
1 특정한
2 사진
3 좌석
4 약한, 힘이 없는
5 ~을 알고 있는
6 파괴하다
7 왕국
8 탐사하다, 탐험하다
9 법
10 위, 복부, 배
11 자세히 말하다, 묘사하다
12 찾다, 찾아보다

B
1 language
2 Suddenly
3 magazine
4 victory
5 match
6 pity
7 average
8 donate
9 secret
10 author

ⓒ 1 O 2 O 3 O 4 X 5 X

ⓓ 1 magazine 잡지
2 law 법
3 kingdom 왕국
4 secret 비밀
5 inform 알리다
6 match 어울리다, 성냥
7 donate 기증하다, 기부하다
8 aware ~을 알고 있는
9 language 언어
10 author 작가
11 destroy 파괴하다
12 seat 좌석
13 suddenly 갑자기, 급작스럽게
14 pity 동정심, 안타까움, 유감
15 weak 약한, 힘이 없는
16 fare 요금
17 average 평균의, 보통의, 일반적인
18 stomach 위, 복부, 배
19 within ~ 안에, ~ 이내에
20 craft 공예, 공예품
21 path 길
22 Search 찾다, 찾아보다
23 describe 자세히 말하다, 묘사하다
24 particular 특정한
25 village 마을
26 photograph 사진
27 lock 잠그다, 자물쇠
28 explore 탐사하다, 탐험하다
29 throat 목구멍, 목
30 victory 승리

Lesson 29 **Check Up** ················· **p. 101**

ⓐ • direct — ① 직접적인, 직행의, 지도하다, 감독하다
• probably — ⑥ 아마
• conversation — ⑦ 대화
• seem — ⑤ ~인 것처럼 보이나, ~인 것 같다
• patient — ② 환자, 인내심이 있는
• lay — ⑧ 놓다, 두다
• package — ④ 소포, 꾸러미
• pleasure — ③ 기쁨

ⓑ 1 whale   2 ban
3 tiny   4 mission
5 effect   6 fault
7 suffer

Lesson 30 **Check Up** ················· **p. 103**

ⓐ • medicine — ⑧ 의약품, 의학
• beard — ① 턱수염
• disagree — ⑥ 의견이 다르다, 동의하지 않다
• effort — ③ 노력
• shadow — ② 그림자
• mobile — ④ 이동식의, 이동할 수 있는
• sentence — ⑤ 문장
• personality — ⑦ 성격

ⓑ 1 indoor   2 talent
3 suggest   4 flow
5 sweet   6 tip
7 liberty

Review ················· **pp. 104~105**

ⓐ 1 고래   2 의약품, 의학
3 재능   4 문장
5 ~인 것처럼 보이다, ~인 것 같다 6 실내의
7 아주 작은   8 제안하다
9 흐르다   10 턱수염
11 자유   12 성격

ⓑ 1 conversation   2 direct
3 sweet   4 effect
5 shadow   6 effort
7 patient   8 disagree
9 package   10 probably

ⓒ 1 O 2 X 3 O 4 O 5 X

ⓓ 1 suggest 제안하다
2 liberty 자유
3 talent 재능
4 patient 환자, 인내심이 있는
5 personality 성격
6 pleasure 기쁨
7 effort 노력
8 shadow 그림자
9 fault 잘못, 흠
10 indoor 실내의
11 lay 놓다, 두다
12 suffer 시달리다, 겪다
13 medicine 의약품, 의학
14 sentence 문장
15 direct 직접적인, 직행의, 지도하다, 감독하다

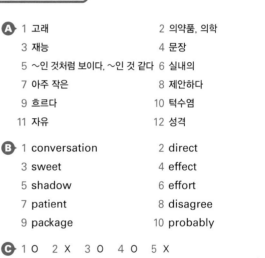

16 whale 고래

17 ban 금지하다

18 sweet 달콤한, 단

19 conversation 대화

20 tip 뾰족한 끝, 조언, 봉사료

21 effect 효과, 영향

22 tiny 아주 작은

23 beard 턱수염

24 mission 임무

25 probably 아마

26 package 소포, 꾸러미

27 disagree 의견이 다르다, 동의하지 않다

28 seem ~인 것처럼 보이다, ~인 것 같다

29 mobile 이동식의, 이동할 수 있는

30 flow 흐르다

누적 테스트 450 ·········· pp. 106~109

A
1 접다
2 의상, 복장
3 의견
4 소음
5 싸다
6 얼룩, 반점, 장소
7 흔들리다, 흔들다
8 간단한, 단순한
9 전문가
10 평균의, 보통의, 일반적인
11 소리를 지르다, 외치다
12 환경
13 길
14 기분이 상한
15 삼키다
16 가장 중요한, 주된
17 심각한, 진지한
18 잘못, 흠
19 모양, 형태
20 그림자
21 요리법, 레시피
22 수준, 단계
23 마을
24 상상하다
25 거르다, 빼먹다

26 count
27 throw
28 result
29 law
30 toe
31 terrible
32 perfect
33 billion
34 author
35 victory
36 flat
37 explain
38 tiny
39 shoulder
40 sweet
41 beard
42 thumb
43 balance
44 symbol
45 trust
46 rule
47 mistake
48 fare
49 benefit
50 tear

B
1 review
3 blanket
5 tool

2 stream
4 report
6 expensive

7 package
9 arrest
11 highway
13 public
15 nervous
17 available
19 continue
21 Though
23 excellent
25 search

8 offer
10 comfortable
12 athlete
14 rope
16 Suddenly
18 seat
20 hammer
22 international
24 except

C
1 prefer
3 donated
5 purpose
7 serves
9 effort
11 votes
13 local
15 temperature
17 dictionary
19 effect
21 silent
23 attend
25 loud

2 toward
4 chasing
6 similar
8 rude
10 banned
12 Knock
14 ordinary
16 indoor
18 flows
20 complained
22 pile
24 produced

D
1 patience 인내
2 apology 사과
3 delivery 배달
4 decoration 장식
5 please 기쁘게 하다
6 anxiety 걱정, 근심
7 decide 결정하다
8 sudden 갑작스러운
9 response 반응
10 description 묘사
11 creative 창의적인
12 particularly 특별히, 특히
13 information 정보
14 painful 아픈, 고통스러운
15 protection 보호

INDEX

중학 영단어 시리즈

VOCA 탄탄

2
기본

저자   Ronnie Kim

초판 1쇄 발행 2017년 10월 1일
초판 3쇄 발행 2022년 2월 24일

편집장   조미자
책임편집   최수경·류은정·김미경·정진희·권민정
표지디자인   디자인 섬
디자인   디자인 섬·임미영
인쇄   삼화 인쇄

펴낸이   정규도
펴낸곳   Happy House, an imprint of DARAKWON

주소   경기도 파주시 문발로 211 다락원 빌딩
전화   02-736-2031 (내선 250)
팩스   02-732-2037
출판등록   1977년 9월 16일 제406-2008-000007호

ISBN 978-89-6653-544-6   53740

값 11,000원

구성 본책+워크북
무료 다운로드 Answers, Daily Test, MP3 파일 ㅣ **www.ihappyhouse.co.kr**
문제출제 프로그램 voca.ihappyhouse.co.kr
*Happy House는 다락원의 임프린트입니다.

중학 영단어 시리즈

VOCA
탄탄 (WORKBOOK)

2
기본

Happy House

VOCA 탄탄

2

기본

WORKBOOK

다음 영어단어의 우리말을 쓰고 단어를 반복하여 쓰시오.

	우리말	영어단어
among	전	
	The band is popular ( ) teenagers.	
shoulder	명	
	My dad has broad ( )s.	
shape	명	
	These blocks are all different ( )s.	
wise	형	
	Always try to make ( ) decisions.	
snake	명	
	There are various ( )s in this desert.	
accept	동	
	Ms. Turner decided to ( ) the offer.	
trouble	명	
	I'm having ( ) with my homework.	
shake	동	
	( ) the juice before you drink it.	
pole	명	
	It is coldest at the South ( ).	
serious	형	
	Kevin never tells jokes. He is always ( ).	
tongue	명	
	I burned my ( ) on the hot soup.	
beg	동	
	A man was ( )ging for money on the street.	
fortunately	부	
	( ), I made no mistakes on the exam.	
physical	형	
	Is ( ) appearance important for success?	
parade	명	
	Some bands are participating in the ( ).	

다음 영어단어의 우리말을 쓰고 단어를 반복하여 쓰시오.

	우리말	영어단어
asleep	⑱	
	I fell ( ) during the movie.	
mistake	⑲	
	Everybody can make a ( ).	
midnight	⑲	
	Lauren woke up suddenly at ( ).	
without	㉙	
	You cannot succeed ( ) their help.	
pair	⑲	
	How many ( )s of socks do you have?	
active	⑱	
	I'm an ( ) member of this club.	
environment	⑲	
	What should we do to save our ( )?	
main	⑱	
	What is the ( ) idea of the book?	
polite	⑱	
	It is not ( ) to whisper in front of others.	
order	⑲ ⑧	
	I'd like to ( ) a pepperoni pizza.	
upset	⑱	
	Sometimes small things make us ( ).	
behavior	⑲	
	Emily apologized for her bad ( ).	
gentle	⑱	
	The man's smile was ( ) and soft.	
item	⑲	
	Some ( )s are displayed in the shop window.	
swallow	⑧	
	( ) the pills at once.	

다음 영어단어의 우리말을 쓰고 단어를 반복하여 쓰시오.

	우리말	영어단어
noise	명	
	Do not make ( ) in the library.	
mud	명	
	His boots were covered with ( ).	
simple	형	
	The recipe for popcorn is very ( ).	
able	형	
	Some birds are not ( ) to fly.	
plus	전 접	
	One ( ) two is three.	
announce	동	
	The winner of the contest will be ( )d soon.	
experience	동 명	
	Ms. Brown has a lot of teaching ( ).	
manner	명	
	Greet the guests in a friendly ( ).	
shout	동	
	My sister ( )ed at me to be quiet.	
shade	명	
	A man is sleeping under the ( ) of a tree.	
envelope	명	
	Sam put some pictures in the ( ).	
thief	명	
	A ( ) stole my purse.	
goods	명	
	The brand is known for its leather ( ).	
position	명	
	The moon changes ( )s from night to night.	
total	형 명	
	This book has a ( ) of 200 pages.	

다음 영어단어의 우리말을 쓰고 단어를 반복하여 쓰시오.

	우리말	영어단어
pan	명	
	I used a frying ( ) to cook the bacon.	
nest	명	
	Some birds make their ( )s in the tree tops.	
orchestra	명	
	Kevin plays cello in the school ( ).	
alive	형	
	The bug is not dead. It's ( ).	
prefer	동	
	Which do you ( ), coffee or tea?	
attention	명	
	Pay ( ) when you walk across the street.	
explain	동	
	Can you ( ) why you're late?	
mark	동 명	
	I ( )ed my name on the book cover.	
possible	형	
	Is it ( ) to buy the book online?	
limit	동 명	
	Do not drive faster than the speed ( ).	
trust	동 명	
	Ellen is always honest, so you can ( ) her.	
billion	명	
	This world's population is over seven ( ).	
grab	동	
	Please ( ) your bag and follow me.	
president	명	
	Karen is the ( ) of our book club.	
treasure	명	
	The boy found hidden ( )s under the tree.	

다음 영어단어의 우리말을 쓰고 단어를 반복하여 쓰시오.

	우리말	영어단어
blow	동	
	A strong wind is ( )ing from the west.	
award	명 동	
	I can't believe that I won the ( )!	
strange	형	
	I had a ( ) dream last night.	
although	접	
	( ) it was raining, we still went out.	
maybe	부	
	( ) Molly didn't tell the truth.	
avoid	동	
	Why are you often ( )ing me?	
favor	명	
	Can I ask you a ( )?	
master	명 동	
	It is not easy to ( ) a foreign language.	
post	동	
	Mr. Turner ( )ed a notice on the wall.	
share	동	
	Jessica ( )s a bedroom with her sister.	
unique	형	
	Everyone has a ( ) fingerprint.	
blossom	명 동	
	Yeouido is famous for its cherry ( )s.	
handle	명 동	
	Turn the ( ) to open the door.	
cancel	동	
	The baseball game was ( )ed because of the weather.	
typical	형	
	( ) teenagers care about their appearance.	

다음 영어단어의 우리말을 쓰고 단어를 반복하여 쓰시오.

	우리말	영어단어
count	동	
	I ( )ed the coins and put them into my pocket.	
occur	동	
	An earthquake can ( ) anywhere on Earth.	
price	명	
	What's the ( ) of the concert ticket?	
argue	동	
	The brothers always ( ) with each other.	
relax	동	
	Let's just sit down and ( ) for a minute.	
balance	명 동	
	It can be difficult to ( ) on one leg.	
few	형	
	There are ( ) students at school on weekends.	
matter	명 동	
	It doesn't ( ) who will go there.	
praise	동 명	
	The teacher ( )d Leah for her kindness.	
shine	동	
	Millions of stars are ( )ing brightly in the sky.	
tough	형	
	This meat is too ( ). I can't eat it.	
border	명	
	Niagara Falls is on the ( ) of Canada and America.	
harm	명 동	
	The drought did great ( ) to the crops.	
provide	동	
	We ( )d poor people with food and clothes.	
reason	명	
	The baby started crying without any ( )s.	

다음 영어단어의 우리말을 쓰고 단어를 반복하여 쓰시오.

	우리말	영어단어
pond	명	
	The ( ) is very deep. Don't swim there.	
outdoor	형	
	I like ( ) activities like trekking.	
spend	동	
	I ( ) more than 100 dollars on shoes.	
arrow	명	
	Follow the ( )s to the event spot.	
reply	명 동	
	You must ( ) to the letter right now.	
bark	동	
	My dog only ( )s at strangers.	
flash	명 동	
	I just saw a ( ) of lightning.	
mayor	명	
	Who is the ( ) of your city?	
prepare	동	
	My mom ( )d meals for us.	
pollution	명	
	Air ( ) is a serious problem in China.	
volume	명	
	Please turn up the ( ) on the TV.	
bother	동	
	Don't ( ) to pick me up at the airport.	
horror	명	
	Joshua loves ( ) movies about ghosts.	
purpose	명	
	What's the ( ) of your visit?	
usual	형	
	I arrived at school earlier than ( ).	

다음 영어단어의 우리말을 쓰고 단어를 반복하여 쓰시오.

	우리말	영어단어
degree	명	
	The temperature this morning is 17 ( )s.	
own	동 형	
	Everyone has his or her ( ) personality.	
stick	명 동	
	The old man uses a ( ) to walk.	
attack	동 명	
	A lion is ( )ing zebras.	
rhythm	명	
	Let's dance to the ( ) of the music.	
beat	동 명	
	Nicole ( ) me in the race.	
flat	형	
	Some people still believe that the Earth is ( ).	
mechanic	명	
	The ( ) is checking the engine of a car.	
privacy	명	
	We should respect other people's ( ).	
silent	형	
	The stage became dark and ( ).	
volunteer	명 동	
	Many ( )s gathered to clean up the park.	
bullet	명	
	There are some ( ) holes in the wall.	
ignore	동	
	Heather ( )d her mom's advice.	
quality	명 형	
	The store sells ( ) products.	
vehicle	명	
	There are always many ( )s on that road.	

다음 영어단어의 우리말을 쓰고 단어를 반복하여 쓰시오.

	우리말	영어단어
drawer	명	
	My desk ( )s are full of school supplies.	
bin	명	
	I threw the socks into the laundry ( ).	
still	부	
	I ( ) remember my first day at elementary school.	
rule	명	
	The ( )s of the new game are easy to understand.	
role	명	
	Alex plays an important ( ) in our club.	
blank	형 명	
	Fill in the ( )s with your name and address.	
float	동	
	A balloon is ( )ing in the sky.	
melt	동	
	Chocolate was ( )ing in my fingers.	
process	명 동	
	The ( ) of building a ship is very complex.	
slide	동 명	
	This swimming pool has water ( )s.	
vote	동 명	
	How many ( )s did the new class president get?	
bully	동 명	
	Ethan is being ( )ed by his classmates.	
imagine	동	
	George never ( )d meeting his mom there.	
rather	부	
	That is a ( ) difficult question for me.	
warn	동	
	The teacher ( )ed me not to be late again.	

다음 영어단어의 우리말을 쓰고 단어를 반복하여 쓰시오.

우리말	영어단어
ease	
⑲	
Tyler solved the math questions with (　　　　　).	
past	
⑲ ⑲	
I think people were happier in the (　　　　　).	
storm	
⑲	
Lots of tall trees fell down in the (　　　　　).	
a bit	
Julia moved (　　　　　) closer to me.	
plate	
⑲	
My mom put a piece of cake on my (　　　　　).	
blind	
⑲ ⑲	
These are guide dogs for (　　　　　) people.	
forecast	
⑲ ⑲	
The weather (　　　　　) says it will snow tomorrow.	
mental	
⑲	
The patient has some (　　　　　) problems.	
produce	
⑲	
The factory (　　　　　)s about 1,000 cars a day.	
society	
⑲	
I want big changes in our (　　　　　).	
weigh	
⑲	
The big dog (　　　　　)s over 12kg.	
pretend	
⑲	
I (　　　　　)ed I was sleeping when Dad called me.	
include	
⑲	
Shakespeare's works (　　　　　) *Romeo and Juliet* and *Hamlet*.	
realize	
⑲	
Ian (　　　　　)d that he made a big mistake.	
whole	
⑲	
We spent the (　　　　　) day fishing at the lake.	

다음 영어단어의 우리말을 쓰고 단어를 반복하여 쓰시오.

	우리말	영어단어
hole	명	
	Your right sock has a ( ) in the back.	
pattern	명	
	The dress has a floral ( ).	
sore	형	
	I have a ( ) throat with the flu.	
blanket	명	
	This ( ) will keep you warm.	
sense	명 동	
	Taste is one of the five ( )s.	
breathe	동	
	This room is full of smoke. I can't ( ) here.	
forgive	동	
	Kevin apologized, but I didn't ( ) him.	
million	명	
	Gwangju has around 1.5 ( ) people.	
punish	동	
	I was ( )ed for fighting with my brother.	
grade	명	
	Lily got a poor ( ) on the math exam.	
wheel	명	
	Most vehicles have two or four ( )s.	
capital	명 형	
	The ( ) of Vietnam is Hanoi.	
increase	동 명	
	The population of our country is ( )ing.	
recognize	동	
	The actor wore sunglasses, so no one ( )d him.	
humid	형	
	Indonesia is hot and ( ) most of the year.	

다음 영어단어의 우리말을 쓰고 단어를 반복하여 쓰시오.

우리말	영어단어
fair	형 명 All of us want to play a (　　　　) game.	
pepper	명 Add a little salt and (　　　　) to the steak.	
stretch	동 (　　　　) your arms and legs before you exercise.	
cave	명 Many bats live in the (　　　　).	
sheet	명 Please give me a (　　　　) of paper.	
bride	명 The (　　　　) and groom look very happy.	
fortune	명 Adam had the good (　　　　) to win a lottery.	
miracle	명 It is a (　　　　) that no one was injured in the fire.	
pure	형 Is the medal made of (　　　　) gold?	
spoil	동 The heavy rain (　　　　)ed our picnic.	
wonder	동 I (　　　　) who will win the next World Cup.	
chase	동 A cat is (　　　　)ing after a mouse.	
intelligent	형 Humans are more (　　　　) than other animals.	
regular	형 The music festival became a (　　　　) event.	
underground	형 부 Many trains travel through the (　　　　) tunnel.	

다음 영어단어의 우리말을 쓰고 단어를 반복하여 쓰시오.

우리말	영어단어
final (형)	
What was the ( ) score of today's game?	
piece (명)	
I just ate the last ( ) of the apple pie.	
such (형)(부)	
It's ( ) a beautiful day, isn't it?	
chest (명)	
I have a pain in my ( ).	
shower (명)	
I take a ( ) every morning.	
celebrate (동)	
Let's ( ) our victory!	
spirit (명)	
Yoga can strengthen your body and ( ).	
monster (명)	
Do you believe that a ( ) lives in the lake?	
raise (동)	
Natalie ( )d her hand and asked a question.	
spread (동)	
The flu can ( ) from person to person.	
yell (동)	
My mom never ( )s although she sometimes gets angry.	
cheek (명)	
The woman kissed her baby on the ( ).	
invent (동)	
The light bulb was ( )ed by Thomas Edition.	
remain (동)	
Only five minutes ( ) in the exam.	
survey (명)(동)	
The school took a ( ) of all the students.	

Lesson 14

다음 영어단어의 우리말을 쓰고 단어를 반복하여 쓰시오.

	우리말	영어단어
flood	명 동 The river was ( )ed by the heavy rain.	
fur	명 These coats are made from animal ( ).	
sweat	동 명 Some people ( ) more than others.	
vacation	명 We are looking forward to summer ( ).	
silver	명 Amy finished in second place, so she received the ( ) medal.	
challenge	동 명 Blake ( )d me to a game of ping pong.	
greet	동 The waitress ( )ed us with a big smile.	
muscle	명 Cycling is good for your leg ( )s.	
reach	동 Michelle's hair ( )es her waist.	
stairs	명 I fell down on the ( ) and broke my leg.	
abroad	부 My aunt travels ( ) every summer.	
chin	명 The man wiped his daughter's ( ) with a napkin.	
local	형 There are two ( ) newspapers in our city.	
repair	동 My cellphone isn't working. I need to ( ) it.	
purse	명 Allison took some money out of her ( ).	

다음 영어단어의 우리말을 쓰고 단어를 반복하여 쓰시오.

	우리말	영어단어
pine	명	
	Many squirrels live in the ( ) forest.	
screen	명	
	Don't look at the computer ( ) in the dark.	
wing	명	
	The ostrich has ( )s, but it cannot fly.	
seed	명	
	Most fruits have ( )s inside them.	
since	전 접	
	Ms. Suzuki has lived in Seoul ( ) 2010.	
choir	명	
	The school ( ) practices once a week.	
hall	명	
	The hotel's ( ) can hold 300 people.	
narrow	형	
	Drive carefully because the road is ( ).	
university	명	
	There are many famous ( )es in Boston.	
statue	명	
	The sculptor made the ( ) from marble.	
achieve	동	
	Do everything to ( ) your goal.	
chop	동	
	( ) up some vegetables for a salad.	
loss	명	
	The artist's death was a great ( ) to our country.	
research	명 동	
	The doctor spent his life doing medical ( ).	
nearby	형	
	The injured people were sent to a ( ) hospital.	

다음 영어단어의 우리말을 쓰고 단어를 반복하여 쓰시오.

	우리말	영어단어
guest	명	
	We will have 30 ( )s at the party.	
cure	동 명	
	There is no ( ) for a cold.	
terrible	형	
	I heard some ( ) news yesterday.	
dive	동	
	Don't ( ) into the pool.	
slim	형	
	Nick is ( ), but his brother is fat.	
clap	동	
	The audience ( )ped when the show was over.	
heel	명	
	The shoes are worn down at the ( )s.	
neat	형	
	Always keep your room ( ).	
receive	동	
	I ordered a blue T-shirt but ( )d a black one.	
straight	부 형	
	Go ( ) and you will find the building.	
advertise	동	
	The company ( )d its new product on TV.	
comfortable	형	
	This sofa is more ( ) than that one.	
disappear	동	
	The man ( )ed in the crowd.	
medium	형	
	I like my steak cooked ( ).	
respect	명 동	
	I have ( ) for my grandfather.	

다음 영어단어의 우리말을 쓰고 단어를 반복하여 쓰시오.

	우리말	영어단어
height	몡	
	The ( ) of the building is over 100 meters.	
pop	동	
	A boy ( )ped the balloon with a pin.	
through	전	
	A woman is walking ( ) the woods.	
dot	몡	
	Connect all the ( )s to find the picture.	
soil	몡	
	Plants need ( ), water, and sunlight to live.	
complain	동	
	Some customers ( )ed about their food.	
hesitate	동	
	If you have any questions, don't ( ) to ask.	
necessary	형	
	A passport is ( ) to travel abroad.	
recommend	동	
	A friend of mine ( )ed this movie to me.	
strike	동	
	Lightning ( ) a tall pine tree last night.	
aisle	몡	
	You can find the eggs at the end of the ( ).	
community	몡	
	The doctor is very famous in this ( ).	
disappoint	동	
	I'm ( )ed with your behavior.	
metal	몡	
	Iron is one of the most widely used ( )s.	
row	몡	
	About 30 people are lined up in a ( ).	

Lesson 18

다음 영어단어의 우리말을 쓰고 단어를 반복하여 쓰시오.

우리말	영어단어
excuse 동 명	
Please ( ) me for being rude.	
poster 명	
A man is putting up ( )s on the wall.	
tie 동 명	
Jane ( )d her dog to a tree for a moment.	
enemy 명	
France and Germany were ( )es for a long time.	
soldier 명	
Millions of ( )s died in the First World War.	
complete 동 형	
It took two hours to ( ) the work.	
household 명	
Almost every ( ) has a computer.	
nervous 형	
I get ( ) when I speak in public.	
reduce 동	
We need to ( ) food waste.	
structure 명	
We will build a huge steel ( ).	
allow 동	
The security guard didn't ( ) us to enter the building.	
compare 동	
I ( )d two skirts and bought one.	
discount 명 동	
Book early and get a ( ).	
modern 형	
The new building looks ( ) and beautiful.	
rumor 명	
According to the ( ), the factory will be closed soon.	

다음 영어단어의 우리말을 쓰고 단어를 반복하여 쓰시오.

	우리말	영어단어
ill	형	
	I felt ( ) yesterday but fine today.	
speech	명	
	His ( ) was very boring.	
tired	형	
	I was very ( ), so I went to bed early.	
equal	형	
	I cut the apple pie into six ( ) pieces.	
square	명 형	
	We bought a ( ) table.	
confident	형	
	I'm ( ) of your success.	
hug	동 명	
	I ( )ged my mom when she came home.	
nod	동	
	The teacher ( )ded when I gave the right answer.	
relieve	동	
	A massage can help ( ) tension.	
sunshine	명	
	Too much ( ) may cause sunburn.	
amazing	형	
	The man is an ( ) dancer.	
confuse	동	
	Words like *lay* and *lie* always ( ) me.	
edge	명	
	The boy is sitting on the ( ) of the sofa.	
native	형 명	
	Mr. McLean is a ( ) of Australia.	
separate	형 동	
	( ) the egg yolk from the white.	

다음 영어단어의 우리말을 쓰고 단어를 반복하여 쓰시오.

	우리말	영어단어
instead	부	
	The white caps were sold out, so I bought a grey one (　　　　).	
protect	동	
	We should (　　　　) our eyes from the sun.	
title	명	
	I can't remember the (　　　　) of the movie.	
flight	명	
	The (　　　　) for Rome will leave at 11 a.m.	
stamp	명	
	Lily has many (　　　　)s in her passport.	
contact	명 동	
	Please (　　　　) us if you need more information.	
improve	동	
	His health is (　　　　)ing day by day.	
officer	명	
	Navy (　　　　)s wear white uniforms and caps.	
respond	동	
	William didn't (　　　　) to my email.	
surface	명	
	The (　　　　) of the Moon looks very rocky.	
amount	명	
	Most elephants eat a large (　　　　) of food.	
continent	명	
	There are five oceans and seven (　　　　)s on Earth.	
education	명	
	Many countries offer free (　　　　) to students.	
normal	형	
	It is (　　　　) to use chopsticks to eat in Korea.	
sight	명	
	A rainbow over the sea is a very beautiful (　　　　).	

다음 영어단어의 우리말을 쓰고 단어를 반복하여 쓰시오.

우리말	영어단어

joke
명
동
Everybody laughed at my ( ).

public
명
형
We can use the ( ) library for free.

toward
전
Most plants grow ( ) the sunlight.

fold
동
( ) your T-shirts and put them in the drawer.

stream
명
The ( ) flows into a larger river.

costume
명
Sam wore ghost ( )s on Halloween.

throw
동
( ) the dice to start the game.

opinion
명
In my ( ), Alice is very smart.

result
명
동
I wasn't happy with the test ( ).

switch
명
동
Which ( ) is for the light?

anxious
형
Mr. Scott is ( ) about losing his hair.

continue
동
The rain ( )d to fall today.

emotion
명
We can express ( )s through gestures.

notice
동
명
The event was canceled without any ( ).

silly
형
I won't answer such a ( ) question.

다음 영어단어의 우리말을 쓰고 단어를 반복하여 쓰시오.

	우리말	영어단어
lead	동	
	This road ( )s to the shopping area.	
recipe	명	
	Can you give me the ( ) for the soup?	
trade	명 동	
	The company ( )s their products mostly in Europe.	
hammer	명	
	Use the ( ) to drive the nails.	
thick	형	
	This book is too ( ) to hold with one hand.	
courage	명	
	I didn't have the ( ) to say "no."	
interesting	형	
	It is always ( ) to go to new places.	
ordinary	형	
	Van Gogh painted mostly ( ) people.	
review	동 명	
	Jamie wrote a book ( ) on his blog.	
symbol	명	
	The eagle was the ( ) of ancient Rome.	
apologize	동	
	Taylor ( )d to us for being late.	
creature	명	
	What is the biggest ( ) on Earth?	
equipment	명	
	You need special ( ) to scuba dive.	
offer	동 명	
	Jacob ( )ed to help me with the homework.	
similar	형	
	My sister and I don't look ( ) at all.	

다음 영어단어의 우리말을 쓰고 단어를 반복하여 쓰시오.

	우리말	영어단어
level	명	
	My Spanish ( ) is not very high.	
record	명 동	
	The athlete broke the world ( ).	
trick	명 동	
	My brother often plays ( )s on me.	
harvest	명 동	
	Some farmers are ( )ing their fields.	
though	접 부	
	Julie likes singing. She is not a good singer ( ).	
dictionary	명	
	A ( ) shows the meaning of a word.	
international	형	
	My brother has an ( ) driver's license.	
pain	명	
	Because of the ( ) in my tooth, I went to a dentist.	
roll	동	
	Some coins ( )ed under the sofa.	
task	명	
	I need more time to complete the ( ).	
arrest	동	
	The police officers ( )ed the man for stealing a car.	
curl	동 명	
	The girl has long brown ( )s.	
excellent	형	
	Mr. Rooney was an ( ) soccer player.	
serve	동	
	The restaurant ( )s traditional Korean food.	
situation	명	
	The ( ) is getting worse and worse.	

다음 영어단어의 우리말을 쓰고 단어를 반복하여 쓰시오.

	우리말	영어단어
lift	동	
	I can't ( ) this box. It's too heavy.	
report	동 / 명	
	The news ( )ed that a big fire broke out yesterday.	
twin	명 / 형	
	The ( )s look very similar.	
highway	명	
	Traffic jams often occur on the ( ).	
thumb	명	
	I slammed my ( ) in the door.	
create	동	
	An artist is ( )ing a sculpture.	
pile	명	
	There is a ( ) of papers on the desk.	
palm	명	
	The dog put its foot on my ( ).	
royal	형	
	We watched the ( ) wedding on TV.	
tear	명 / 동	
	Why were his eyes filled with ( )s?	
athlete	명	
	Thousands of ( )s compete in the Olympic Games.	
decision	명	
	We should make a ( ) quickly.	
except	전	
	The library is open daily ( ) Mondays.	
pace	명	
	Karl walks at a fast ( ).	
skip	동	
	I want to ( ) my piano lesson today.	

다음 영어단어의 우리말을 쓰고 단어를 반복하여 쓰시오.

	우리말	영어단어
list	명	
	Please check if my name is on the waiting ( ).	
ride	동	
	My dad usually ( )s a bus to work.	
clinic	명	
	Call the dental ( ) to make an appointment.	
knight	명	
	The ( )s fought bravely for their king.	
toe	명	
	I broke my ( ) during a soccer game.	
deliver	동	
	Your sofa will be ( )ed tomorrow.	
journal	명	
	I keep a ( ) every day.	
peel	동 명	
	Emma is ( )ing some potatoes in the kitchen.	
rude	형	
	It is ( ) to keep others waiting.	
temperature	명	
	The ( ) of the desert is very high.	
attend	동	
	Children ( ) elementary schools at the age of eight.	
decorate	동	
	Alex ( )d the cake with strawberries.	
expensive	형	
	This computer is more ( ) than that one.	
pack	동	
	Can you help me ( ) the suitcase?	
spot	명	
	The dog has black ( )s on its back.	

다음 영어단어의 우리말을 쓰고 단어를 반복하여 쓰시오.

	우리말	영어단어
loud	형	
	A child is crying in a ( ) voice.	
rope	명	
	Some sailors are pulling the ( ).	
view	명	
	I have a different ( ) from you.	
knock	동	
	( ) on the door before you come in.	
tool	명	
	The mechanic used some ( )s to fix the car.	
determine	동	
	We were ( )d to change some of the rules.	
judge	명 동	
	( )s should always be fair.	
perfect	형	
	The pianist's performance was ( ).	
scare	동	
	The horror story ( )d all of us.	
benefit	명	
	What is the ( ) of reading books?	
available	형	
	Delivery service is not ( ) now.	
delight	명 동	
	The woman received the gift with ( ).	
expert	명	
	Most ( )s expected the German soccer team to win.	
panic	명 동	
	The fire caused a ( ) in the building.	
steam	명	
	( ) is coming out of the kettle.	

Lesson 27

다음 영어단어의 우리말을 쓰고 단어를 반복하여 쓰시오.

	우리말	영어단어
magazine	명 I usually read fashion ( )s.	
author	명 The ( ) wrote many fantasy novels.	
village	명 My grandfather lives in a small ( ).	
law	명 By ( ), you can't smoke in public places.	
victory	명 The player did his best to get a ( ).	
craft	명 The small town is known for its glass ( )s.	
kingdom	명 The queen ruled the ( ) for 20 years.	
photograph	명 I have a ( ) of my family in my wallet.	
search	동 The police are ( )ing for the missing boy.	
throat	명 I have a sore ( ) and cough.	
average	형 What is the ( ) temperature here?	
describe	동 The woman ( )d her experience in Sweden.	
explore	동 The divers are ( )ing the underwater cave.	
particular	형 Is there any ( ) item you are looking for?	
stomach	명 My ( ) is full. I can't eat any more food.	

다음 영어단어의 우리말을 쓰고 단어를 반복하여 쓰시오.

우리말	영어단어
match 동 명	
This necklace ( )es your dress.	
seat 명	
I was in the front ( ) in the theater.	
weak 형	
I feel a little ( ) today.	
lock 동 명	
Sometimes I forget to ( ) the door.	
within 전	
I'll get there ( ) an hour.	
donate 동	
A rich man ( )d 10 million dollars.	
language 명	
Chen's native ( ) is Chinese.	
pity 명	
It's a ( ) that you can't join us.	
secret 명	
This is a ( ). Can you keep it?	
inform 동	
Please ( ) us of any change in the plan.	
aware 형	
I wasn't ( ) that my mom was sick.	
destroy 동	
The bomb ( )ed the entire building.	
fare 명	
How much is the subway ( )?	
path 명	
We walked along a narrow ( ).	
suddenly 부	
The field trip was ( ) canceled.	

다음 영어단어의 우리말을 쓰고 단어를 반복하여 쓰시오.

	우리말	영어단어
probably	부	
	The baby is ( ) sleeping now.	
conversation	명	
	Why don't you join in the ( )?	
whale	명	
	Some ( )s are swimming in the ocean.	
mission	명	
	I have a ( ) to complete.	
package	명	
	A mailman left a ( ) for you.	
effect	명	
	Smoking has a bad ( ) on your health.	
lay	동	
	Will you ( ) the magazine on the table?	
pleasure	명	
	It's a ( ) to see you again.	
seem	동	
	The woman ( )ed tired.	
tiny	형	
	The glass broke into ( ) pieces.	
ban	동	
	The school ( )ned using smartphones in class.	
direct	형 동	
	I want a ( ) answer from Amy.	
fault	명	
	Don't worry. It's not your ( ).	
patient	명 형	
	Be ( ) and wait for the result.	
suffer	동	
	I ( )ed from a headache last night.	

다음 영어단어의 우리말을 쓰고 단어를 반복하여 쓰시오.

	우리말	영어단어
medicine	명	
	Take this ( ) three times a day.	
shadow	명	
	The baby was afraid of his own ( ).	
talent	명	
	We were surprised at Anna's musical ( ).	
mobile	형	
	The ( ) library has over 5,000 books.	
indoor	형	
	I like ( ) activities like playing video games.	
effort	명	
	You can't succeed without ( ).	
liberty	명	
	We visited the Statue of ( ) in New York.	
sweet	형	
	My family likes ( ) apple pie.	
sentence	명	
	Make a ( ) with these words.	
tip	명	
	Here are some ( )s for saving money.	
beard	명	
	The old man had a long ( ).	
disagree	동	
	Do you agree or ( ) with the decision?	
flow	동	
	The river ( )s into the Yellow Sea.	
personality	명	
	The girl has a cheerful ( ).	
suggest	동	
	Riley ( )ed going to see a baseball game.	

중학 영단어 시리즈

VOCA
탄탄

2 기본